From Wedding Rings To Imperfect Dreams

MARIA MITCHELL

Memoir

From Wedding Rings to Imperfect Dreams

Copyright © 2020 Maria Mitchell

All rights reserved. No part of this publication may be produced, distributed, or transmitted in any form or by any means, including photocopying, recording, or other electronic or mechanical methods, without the prior written permission of the publisher, except in the case of brief quotations embodied in critical reviews and certain other non-commercial uses permitted by copyright law.

This book is not intended as a substitute for the medical advice of physicians. The reader should regularly consult a physician in matters relating to his / her health and particularly with respect to any symptoms that may require diagnosis or medical attention.

First Printed in United Kingdom 2020

Published by Conscious Dreams Publishing
www.consciousdreamspublishing.com

Edited by Rhoda Molife
www.molahmedia.com

ISBN: 978-1-913674-02-1

MESSAGE FROM THE AUTHOR

Some of you may know that Tyrone had many gifts — one of them was that he was gifted with words. I have the great honour and opportunity to share some of Tyrone's words with you as I share my story.

Although some of what Tyrone has written was prior to our meeting, I'm sure that as you read, you will agree that Tyrone's words are somehow perfectly interlinked with the journey upon which he and I embarked. Some individuals, even those closest to me, do not understand why I have kept his light in my heart. It is because there wouldn't be Maria Mitchell without a Tyrone Mitchell, and there wouldn't be the opportunity to have written From Wedding Rings to Imperfect Dreams.

Tyrone — your life and legacy continues to contribute to my purpose, even from beyond the grave. Once my *T-Mi Rey*, you will always be remembered as a king.

My King, in Loving Memory and Honour of You Today

I wrote this dedication to mark the first year anniversary of Tyrone's graduation into heaven.

The majority of this dedication was written at 3 a.m. a few days ago. I wanted to publish it on the thirtieth; however, I knew I wouldn't be in a stable enough emotional state to put anything tangible together if I wrote it on that day. To be honest, I probably would've decided against writing it. It is really difficult to write about him in this way. Reflecting like this makes the fact that he's not here even rawer — maybe even against human nature. Although my heart hurts really badly, I will continue to write as Tyrone deserved for me to celebrate him — especially today. I can no longer celebrate him in person, but I can honour who he was and his legacy.

So, today is D-Day. Today marks one year since my beloved husband, Tyrone, went to be with his Creator on Wednesday, 30th September 2015. Honestly, I can't even bring myself to write "anniversary", so I won't. Maybe it's just me, but I've always associated the word "anniversary" with a celebration of something positive — you know, meeting your boyfriend or girlfriend for the first time, your first date, his proposal, your wedding, and so on.

Wikipedia defines an anniversary as "a day that commemorates or celebrates a past event that occurred on the same date of the year as the initial event."

I'll take the word "commemorate" and dwell on it.

Today is the day on which I am forced to celebrate Tyrone's life without him physically here. How I feel today (written on the 30th September 2016): People said it would be really painful, and they were right. I woke up not feeling how I imagined or expected to feel. I looked at my phone, saw the date, and let out an "arghh," as if disgusted at discovering the date. I expected to feel teary-eyed as soon as I woke up, but I actually just feel numb. My chest hurt a little, and I felt a little nauseated, but the main feeling was numbness. It felt really surreal, as if it had never happened.

Yesterday, a friend described it as if all of this — Tyrone not being here — is happening in an alternate universe. It hit me in the shower when I realised the time and reflected on the fact that Ty would've been dead by now.

I'm a planner, and I made sure I wouldn't be sitting in the house alone today, so I'm heading out in a few minutes. As random as it may seem, I started the day shortly after midnight, thanking God for Tyrone's life and the fact that I still had the gift of life.

The positives are that he is no longer in pain — he's happy and at complete peace, hanging out in heaven with his Creator. He's probably sparring with Angel Michael, having an eternal debate with King Solomon (I wonder who will win), or challenging King David to a dance-off convinced he'll be the victor. Somehow, he's managed to rope in Abraham, Moses, and Prophet Elijah to be the judges.

I could dwell on the fact that he is no longer here with me — with us; however, I'm going to use this platform instead today to celebrate the awesome man he was. To be his wife was life's greatest honour; it really was! I was smitten with him because I recognised the gift he was to me — to the world. He was the most patient, trustworthy, loving husband and he treated me like a queen every single day. He was my best friend, my confidante, my comrade and my teacher. He had the biggest heart of anyone I knew and he taught me how to love unconditionally. I've always said that he was the best side of me.

My house was really quiet before I met him. He brought so much joy into our house, and because of him, it became a home. He was just so silly, and he made me comfortable enough to join him in his crazy antics. Have you ever heard his laugh? Actually, I wouldn't call it a laugh. It was more like a thunderous roar. I imagine that if giants could laugh, that's how they would sound. Maybe it's how God sounds when he whispers (he definitely inherited that sound from his Creator). It was those unexpected moments when our pastor said something funny (or not) in the middle of church services that it always got to me; it was so loud!

He somehow always got everyone to laugh along with him. I really miss that laugh. He was always so happy and positive about everything — every single thing (that really annoyed me sometimes) His daily mission was to be that light in the dark room. He wanted people to say, "I was having an awful day, but then I came across this big guy called Tyrone and my day changed for the better." To him, life was his greatest gift, and he was determined to live every day to its fullest.

Do you remember his voices and voiceovers he used to do? He had so many, and he did them so well. Do you remember that lip tremble? When someone was talking, and he believed they were chatting rubbish, he would do this stupid bottom lip tremble thing without them noticing, as if to say, "Why are you still chatting? No one believes you (LOL)." It was so stupid that it made everyone laugh; oh, such nonsense! I know his closest friends remember it. Plus, I've witnessed some of you doing it yourselves. Go on — give it a go. You know he'll be watching and cracking up in heaven.

He really did have a powerful gift. I really miss that, too. I know quite a few of us who remember him going out of his way to wind people up. He actually enjoyed being annoying, exposing his friends and leaving people hanging.

His closest friends and family got the brunt of it in public (Don't worry — I had words with him at home about it and he was slightly apologetic). I'm grinning as I write this because it was actually very funny. He hardly exposed me in public — I guess it was because he remembered who he was going home with. We all quickly forgave him because it was Tyrone, and he meant no harm — we loved him even more for it.

He lived to be the person who people say, "There's something really magical about that guy — I want to be around him," when they met him. And people gravitated towards him. God used Tyrone mightily to share His strength, His wisdom and His love with the world.

He loved talking, sharing, talking and debating. If you ever had the privilege of meeting him or knowing him, you would remember the words — oh, the words that would come out of his mouth. He wouldn't talk for the sake of talking. His words were intrinsically and mesmerisingly articulated, full of life and hope and they always seemed expressed at the right time. It was as if Jesus himself were speaking to you. Tyrone was the wisest person I knew. Please, always treasure the words Tyrone spoke to you.

His unrelenting trust in God, I believe, was his greatest gift. I admired this about him the most. He trusted God with every part of life, no matter the season. Even from his hospital bed, he shared the Gospel and God's faithfulness. He taught me it was okay to give without having much because even if God didn't bless us (which He did), it was the right thing to do.

Observing this while married to him taught me so many invaluable lessons. To learn to trust God with my whole life, even when beaten, bloodied and messed up and staggering in the wilderness (still a process) and maintaining my faith has been the greatest lesson of it all.

So there it is — a snapshot of what makes Tyrone so special. I know each of you can write your own essays about how awesome he was, the impact he had on your lives and how he challenged and changed each of your lives for the better. For those of you that never had the priceless privilege of meeting and knowing him, hopefully, you'll catch a glimpse of his awesomeness through me or by hearing the countless stories that continue to be told about him and his legacy.

That's it for now, guys, but let's remember that even though Tyrone is no longer here in person, he remains forever in our hearts and that is irreplaceable. He loved all of us with the same love as Jesus. We will forever love him and we thank him for choosing to spend his life with us. I am forever grateful to God for creating him and giving him to me as my husband. It was life's greatest honour and privilege to know and love him. I am grateful to have had that special role as his wife and that he chose to share and spend the rest of his life with me. I am a better person and a better woman because of him and I will continue his/our legacy of letting our light shine.

Just like Tyrone, let's always remember what it says in 1 Corinthians 9:24-27 (The Message version):

You've all been to the stadium and seen the athlete's race. Everyone runs; one wins. Run to win. All good athletes train hard. They do it for a gold medal that tarnishes and fades. You're after one that's gold eternally. I don't know about you, but I'm running hard for the finish line. I'm giving it everything I've got. No sloppy living for me! I'm staying alert and in top condition. I'm not going to get caught napping, telling everyone else all about it, and then missing out myself.

I came across this stunning quote shortly after Tyrone's passing and it is definitely something to keep in mind: "What the caterpillar perceives is the end,to the butterfly is just the beginning" (Author unknown).

To my beautiful Tyrone Anthony Ian Mitchell:
we will love and cherish you for all eternity!
24/11/1986 – 30/09/2015

TABLE OF CONTENTS

Message From the Author.. 3
My King, in Loving Memory and Honour of You Today................. 5
Chapter 1: Call and Response.. 17
Chapter 2: The Promise... 19
Chapter 3: Wedding Rings.. 21
Chapter 4: The Journey Begins 25
Chapter 5: Touched by an Angel 29
Chapter 6: My World's End 33
Personal Musings: From Wedding Rings to Imperfect Dreams.. 37
Chapter 7: The Hospital Room... 41
Chapter 8: We're Still Standing! 45
Chapter 9: We Are Not Afraid of Death! 47
Personal Musings: Do You Believe That I Am a Good Father? ... 49
Chapter 10: My Final Stand 53
Chapter 11: Tyrone's Final Stand 55
Chapter 12: Heavenly Graduation 57
Chapter 13: I Will Get Up!.. 61
Chapter 14: The Audacity of Life... 63
Personal Musings: My Love has Nowhere to Go 65
Chapter 15: Time, Death and Love — My Nemesis 67
Personal Musings: Into my Daddy's Arms 71
Chapter 16: I Am Not a Widow!... 75
Chapter 17: I Have Concluded that God is Still Faithful................ 79
Chapter 18: A Widow's Call 85
Personal Musings: From Pain to Purpose —
    Story of a Modern-day Ruth 97
Chapter 19: Tyrone's Dream — The Parable within Parables 99
Closing Dedication 101
Epilogue: My Love Letter to the Widow 103
Acknowledgements.. 109
Author Bio... 123

FOREWORD

When my dear friend, Maria, asked me to write the foreword to this book, there was absolutely no way I could say no. You see, for the last eight years, I have had the pleasure of journeying with Maria through the many stages of life she describes in this book.

When I first met Maria, I was instantly struck by how calm yet strong her spirit was. Her quiet yet confident demeanour spoke volumes to me. I don't quite remember the exact moment, but we quickly became friends. *Real friends.* Maria is a ride-till-the-wheels-fall-off kind of girl and she has always gone over and above for the people and things she loves.

From being a single woman to meeting and dating Tyrone to getting engaged and married, and then painfully losing the love of her life, there has been a common thread throughout Maria's life: an anchored faith in God and His promises.

I say, "anchored", because, oh, yes, Maria's faith has been shaken, rocked and swayed from side to side, but it has never strayed or moved in its position. Witnessing Maria's strength and perseverance has been a massive inspiration to me and many others. The journey has been long and often tumultuous, but in life, love and loss, Maria has stood firm. She has made sure that her experiences over the past five years have not been in vain — through sharing her story via blogging, speaking events, radio shows and now this incredible book.

I couldn't be more excited about this project because it is truly needed. At a time where so many of us around the world are facing uncertainty, pain, loss and confusion, this book is a beacon of hope. A hope that whatever happens at whatever age or stage in life, we are held by God and there is more after what ultimately seems like the end. As cliché as it may sound, there is always purpose in pain.

Renée Davis

PREFACE

"You have such a powerful story," they said. "You have a gift," they said. "You have to write a book," they said. These were all lovely compliments, but truth be told, I did not want to write a book about my journey. I was content with writing blog posts once in a while.

You see, I have no issue with writing a book. I actually commenced writing a book in 2000, three titles to date with the plan to specifically publish one before I was married. Then, life happened — I met the man of my dreams, we got engaged and we married, all before I had the chance to complete the book. In the back of my mind, I knew I would eventually go back to writing one day, but it was not a priority. I was happy just being a newlywed and commencing the very precious and exciting journey of two becoming one.

Since then, the idea of writing a book at some point has never been far from my mind. I knew that, sooner or later, I would complete the book I had started writing. Even when Tyrone became unwell, we frequently discussed writing a book together. We even penned a couple of chapters about our journey when he was diagnosed with cancer through his healing and recovery. Even in the midst of this, we wanted to share hope and the vast magnitude of God's faithfulness with the world.

Fast forward nine months and "life" happened, yet again, completely breaking just about everything in and around me. There was no way that writing a book was anywhere near my heart or mind. Even after I obeyed God's instruction to start writing blog posts, I never planned to write a book about my journey. Since then, I have had a number of conversations about writing a book with some people who are precious in my life. To them, it was inevitable, and it made sense; however, I refused to move unless instructed to.

Tyrone is no longer present in this life and he will never have the opportunity to share the journey in his words, nor will he share the testimony of his recovery. He is not sitting next to me as I write this preface, nor did he have the opportunity to pen his signature next to mine; however, I am here today as a product of God's love and faithfulness, even in death. I am here today, writing about our journey as Mr. and Mrs. Mitchell and my journey as a Ms.

Yes, I have provided a very in-depth glimpse of this in my blog posts and on social media; however, I have always been prescriptive about what I post as being led by the Holy Spirit. I have listened to that precious voice, which has told me that my story must be told beyond the platforms of social media.

My story, *this story*, is powerful and it needs to reach every corner of the globe. Yes, there are many widows, many young widows, and many Christian young widows; however, there is no one like me, with my experience and my journey. What you read here is different, as I have penned my journey from its embryonic stage to where I find myself today with the sole purpose of inspiring and empowering people from every walk of life and in every season of their lives. I aim to direct your focus on the scarlet thread — Jesus Christ and His blood redemption — which runs through my story and yours. My primary purpose is to shine a light back on the very height, depth and breadth of God's love.

As you turn the pages, come with me as we explore my journey from before I said, "I do," to life after death.

My journey, *From Wedding Rings to Imperfect Dreams.*

CHAPTER 1:
Call and Response

When I share my story, I usually start when I experienced heartbreak in 2012. I vividly remember coming home one evening and going on my knees in the middle of my living room, where I wept and wept. I cried out to God in agony as my heart shattered. I said to God that I never wanted to experience that kind of heartbreak again and I was ready to surrender my heart, my life, and my very being to Him; everything was His.

While on my knees, I remember looking up at the ceiling, my face drenched with tears, my hands clasped and saying to God, "Lord, I am here. Empty me and make me a vessel for your work. Remember your promise to use me like you used Joshua to reach those who are deemed unreachable. Make my heart like David's after you."

As a knelt there, I heard a voice as clear as day respond, "Are you sure?!"

I put a question mark *and* an exclamation point as it was not a response, nor was it a question. The tone felt as if it were a challenge, a grave warning and an opportunity to really reflect on what I was requesting. It really scared me.

My response was *yes*. I got up shortly afterward and everything seemed the same. I continued my evening with a new sense of self-sacrifice. I had little understanding of what I had requested from God and I really had a minimal understanding of David's heart in pursuit of God; however, it made sense to me at that moment. Although things appeared to be the same, I knew a powerful exchange had taken place between God and me. Something I could never take back.

Unbeknownst to me, I was about to embark on the most beautiful yet most difficult and sacrificial journey of my life.

CHAPTER 2:

The Promise

As a little girl, Tyrone Anthony Ian Mitchell was the handsome prince I dreamed I would one day marry when I was older. He was my knight in shining armour — the man that would save me from all of life's challenges, including from myself. He was *the* man for which I had prayed and, I asked God that if He was true, He would grant me the greatest of my heart's desire. He was the man I hoped for after each heartbreak. I dreamed, desired, prayed and hoped for Tyrone, yet a part of me didn't believe that a man like him existed, let alone had ever been created. Just like Sarai, Abram's wife in the Bible, I yearned for yet laughed at *The Promise*.

> *In the depths of my heart, all I knew was that*
> *if "He" did exist, I wanted to experience love, purpose,*
> *and eternity with him.*

Tyrone was actually in my life when I made my request to God. He had been invited to my church — El-Shaddai International Christian Centre and had made the church his home. The person who invited Tyrone had been a friend of mine and was staying with me at that time. She had been dating a friend of mine so all four of us would hang out in our home every so often. Who could have known that Tyrone and I would then go on to exchange numbers and begin a friendship over the following months.

What's crazy is that time progressed really quickly when it came to Ty and me. My earliest memories of interacting and spending time with him outside of the church were around March 2012. By July 2012, we were communicating with romantic intentions. We had started to discuss a future with both of us in it together. We became an official couple with the intention of marrying on 31st October 2012.

And the Lord visited Sarah as He had said, and the Lord did for Sarah as He had spoken. For Sarah conceived and bore Abraham a son in his old age, at the set time of which God had spoken to him. — Genesis 21:1-2 NKJV

On that day, God answered my prayer. He had responded to my heart's cry. He had honoured my willingness to sacrifice myself for His purpose. He was created, he existed, he found me and I was his; I had obtained *My Promise*.

CHAPTER 3:

Wedding Rings

I am so grateful that I married a man like Tyrone. As soon as we started dating, we were already talking about engagement. A couple of years prior to meeting Tyrone, I actually had a vision that I would be married in the month of August. I shared this with Tyrone and he listened and took on my words with quiet acceptance.

I wish I could say I was *that* partner, the one who was totally chilled and went with the flow of things, especially in a relationship, but I sure wasn't. We often spoke about our wedding day, marriage, where we might live and the countries around the world where we could develop and have an impact. Because we spoke about it with such intentionality, it cultivated the deep desire for it to happen. Every time we had a date, it was us 'modelling' how I would be treated when we were eventually married. When Tyrone cooked for me, I pictured him as my future husband, creating a masterpiece in our kitchen. How Tyrone interacted and communicated with me left an impression of how I could expect to be treated when we were married. How Tyrone walked alongside me and celebrated me in public indicated how he would demonstrate my value to others.

I had definitely met the man of my dreams, gifted to me to make up for all of my previous heartbreaks. He was the man that loved me as he loved the rib closest to his heart. I was so proud to be in a relationship and building a future with Tyrone.

We built our relationship intentionally, deeply and quickly. Once we started dating, we spoke about the number of children we would have, their personalities and which one of us they would physically resemble. Before I met Tyrone, I was happy to have twins with the possibility of stretching to three children. Somehow, love and hope motivated us to stretch it to four. I recall discussing our future as we made our way to church, something we did on many occasions. We were on the topic of children's names and we decided to propose two names each. With great glee, Tyrone shared that he had been thinking about a name for one of our daughters for a while: Arayah. He interpreted the name to mean a 'ray of hope'. Even before she was physically in our arms, Tyrone was so proud of who she was destined to be and the representation and impact of hope she would have in the world.

One of the many things I loved about my relationship with Tyrone is that we both dreamed, hoped for the future, shared what we expected to see and were confident in what would be birthed in the future.

The day after my 28th birthday, Tyrone shared that he had planned a date for us, which would first require us to get changed at his mum's house before heading out for the night. Thinking back, this was not one of my proudest memories, as I was adamant that Tyrone should have proposed to me by then, especially since it was my birthday. Rather than appreciate the beautiful birthday meal he had prepared for me the night before and the thoughtful day Tyrone had planned for us, I decided to be ungrateful. I chose to be upset with him and accused him of not being serious about me due to his desire to take his time proposing.

Tyrone did his best to reassure me of his total commitment and intentions toward me. I heard his words, but I was not entirely convinced. As we approached his mum's house, I made a decision to enjoy the rest of the day and put on my game face. Tyrone opened the door and I walked into the front room to hear a great roar of "*Surprise!*" and loads of shouting, laughter and clapping. OMG! I'm sure many of you remember me literally turning around and chasing Tyrone onto the steps. I was so overwhelmed, shocked, and grateful. I had no idea he had planned it. I had been ungrateful and made the day to that point so miserable.

I walked back into a room full of family and friends smiling back at me, followed by Tyrone with a proud grin plastered on his face. Honestly, writing about this six years later sets me alight as it was such a beautiful moment in our journey, one that I will never ever forget. I think I once told Tyrone that the last time I recalled having a party was when I was in nursery — to think he took my words and made it a reality for me was such a beautiful gesture; it really was a divine moment. I recall a moment when I stood by the cake table with my back turned to Tyrone, or maybe my eyes were closed — I don't quite remember the exact details. As I turned around, Tyrone's dark brown eyes no longer looked down, but they were looking up at me and he was down on bended knee.

What that really happening? Was I really seeing what I thought I saw? So many thoughts, feelings and emotions ran through my mind. I think I was shaking by that point. Tyrone opened his hand and in it was a small box. My heart raced. He opened the box and there was a stunning single diamond glaring back at me.

"Maria Oluwagbemisola Olanrewaju Olupeka," he said, "will you do me the honour of being my wife?"

Loud cheers and applause erupted when Tyrone correctly pronounced my lengthy Nigerian name and I was, once again, surprised. How could I say anything but yes to the magnificent man staring at me? As we danced and chatted intimately in the middle of the room, Tyrone quietly asked when I wanted to get married. My heart was overjoyed. I felt a calm acceptance, fully reassured that my dream and my desire to become his wife was going to happen. I looked at Tyrone in shock and he went on to ask if I would be happy to get married that August. I looked at him in awe as the personification of God's love for me. How was he able to top everything else that he had made happen that day? What had I done to deserve a king like him? Even in my failures, he went out of his way to honour us, to honour my heart. Not only had he remembered the vision I had shared with him, but he had chosen to make it a reality for me.

I whispered, "Yes. *Yes*, let's get married!"

A whirlwind thirteen weeks later, and I was standing at the entrance of the Hippodrome in my twisted strap, Grecian chiffon wedding gown next to my older brother. Our ten beautiful bridesmaids in coral strapless dresses accompanied our nine groomsmen in strapping charcoal suits and coral bow ties, preceded by the precious children in our lives. Before I took my first step, my maid of honour looked at me and whispered 'Are you okay?' I inhaled and nodded. I was so nervous as I walked down the aisle to one of my pastors singing *Because of Who You Are*, by Vicki Yohe, trying to keep my focus on the front of the church, doing my best not to miss the timing of the next step.

A few moments later, we were standing hand in hand and I was being pronounced Mrs. Maria Oluwagbemisola Olanrewaju Mitchell. Friday, 23rd of August, 2013 — the day my whole heart, mind and soul was complete and I was full; Tyrone and I were now married.

CHAPTER 4:

The Journey Begins

The journey of a thousand miles always begins with that one brave step. — Tyrone Mitchell

I remember waking up on my wedding day with tears in my eyes. Of course, the romantic thing to say would be that I was overwhelmed with gladness, having officially received my promise, but this was not true. Mate, I was scared! I was actually frightened that my perfect dream had actually come true. Yes, I know it might not make much sense, but maybe those who recall the day after their wedding can relate. You know, sometimes we get so used to hoping for something that takes a long time to come true, or we're stung by disappointment if it doesn't come to pass, but when it actually does, when God actually shocks you, it can be overwhelming and you feel scared and apprehensive of the fact that it is actually here.

I had a mixture of all of these feelings and it hit me that I was actually a *wife*. I was actually there to serve my husband in every sense of the word. My body no longer belonged to me. My ordered life no longer existed with only me — I had another human being to love (I'll share more about my perceived ordered life a little later). I guess I was really overwhelmed by the idea and I perceived the sacrifice of marriage, my accountability to myself, Tyrone, the community, and most importantly, to God, as a life-long commitment. I believe that was what had scared me.

I remember sharing some of this with Tyrone (I chose not to share all of it with him) and embrace the journey as it was meant to be a positive one. Marriage is positive. Being the sweet man he was, he just wiped the tears that fell on my cheeks, held me close and told me that he loved me. He said he was forever mine and I was his as we embarked on this new journey together.

So many memories come to me as I write this. Writing this chapter is harder than I thought it would be. I can write about so much that happened in our marriage; however, I'm going to focus on the parts of our wedding journey that are important for you to grasp.

One thing I must say is that I loved living with Ty. Although he was no stranger to the house when he moved in with me, it was different being there as husband and wife. I loved the process of him moving in his things, cuddling up to him on the sofa and munching (that's really all we did, which is why we put on so much weight in a small amount of time). I loved his gigantic, loud voice and his crazy dances to a different dancehall tune every day, but what I loved the best was knowing that I wasn't alone in this world. Up to that point, I felt as if I really was alone. I now had a best friend in Tyrone.

Tyrone wasn't just a husband to me — he became a father figure. This may seem strange to some, but I never had a father figure growing up and my understanding of — and experience with — my father wasn't positive. Tyrone showed me the love a father should shower on his daughter through comfort and encouragement. He also corrected my behaviour when I was slightly off-key. It was a love I never received from my own father.

Tyrone was the best friend and confidante I always wanted while growing up, that one friend to whom I could entrust my heart, the friend who is your greatest cheerleader. I had some relationships and dated a few guys; however, we never really cultivated a *true* friendship. To be honest, the relationships I developed were founded in my need to be noticed, desired and accepted. Although I met and kissed a few princes among the

Chapter 4: The Journey Begins

many frogs I met, deep down, I always knew the foundations upon which the relationships were built were unstable. Many were the times I tried to convince myself that what I was experiencing was true love, but I always knew it wasn't God's best for me. I wasn't after the perfect man, but I was aware that the man I would marry would love me — all of me!

Tyrone's commitment and loyalty to me as a friend was tested on many occasions. When Tyrone and I were engaged, I shared a burden I'd been carrying for many years with a dear friend of mine. She was the first person with whom I ever shared it. I wanted to share it with Tyrone before we were married however, I was afraid it would change his thoughts and impressions of me and I feared he would end our engagement. My friend encouraged me to tell him, saying, "If he truly loves you and is committed to you now, your sharing won't change that. Trust him to show up for you." So, I shared it with him. As I wept — both as a release and out of the fear I might lose him (I also expressed this fear to him) — he held me, told me that he loved me and reassured me that he wasn't going anywhere. He told me that my sincerity and vulnerability were beautiful, and it was something he would do his best to cover and protect.

At that moment, I knew I had been given a precious gift, not only of a lover but also of a best friend.

One of the earliest challenges in our marriage came when Tyrone suddenly faced redundancy in his newly appointed role in finance. The realisation that he was unable to provide for me financially by bringing income into the family home really rocked him. I am not a man, so I could not fully comprehend the impact this had on him however, I saw how much it grieved him. Tyrone saw this as a direct attack on his masculinity. I know the thoughts that ran through his mind — *'How have I found myself in the position of being newly married and unable to provide for my family?'* How would we save for our already delayed honeymoon?' *'How would my wife see me now? 'Even if she doesn't show with her emotions and actions, would she see me as less of a man?'*

I suggested Tyrone apply for a Jobseeker's Allowance and I shared my experience applying for it. He was not against it, but he, once again, was disappointed in himself and the circumstances. With my full support, Tyrone was able to process this and we navigated that season with strength and grace. It was a season that ended with us celebrating our honeymoon and first-year wedding anniversary in sunny Orlando, Florida. We returned refreshed and danced as celebrants into our second year of marriage. We were so excited to build our future together without the previous year's challenges. Just one year into our journey as a married couple, we had grown together and we were assured that the worst was behind us. It was now our season to lay the foundations of our legacy. We had been equipped with the *Power to Create*, and it was now our *Time to Move*.[1]

---

1 Power to Create and Time to Move were Maria's and Tyrone's businesses

CHAPTER 5:

Touched by an Angel

I remember being in the bedroom one evening with Tyrone. He started coughing as he did, and all of a sudden, he jumped up and rushed to the bathroom sink where he started vomiting violently. It was something he did quite frequently by then and it wrenched my heart to see and hear him in such pain and discomfort. By that point, Tyrone vomited up most of the food he ate and he was losing weight rapidly. He was also exhausted as he wasn't sleeping well because his constant coughing made it difficult to lie down comfortably.

Tyrone had to sleep sitting up in bed with his head and back against the wall while I laid down. It is only now as I write this that I reflect on how emotionally challenging and physically difficult it must have been for Tyrone to observe me lying down to sleep while he sat up every night. By that particular night, Tyrone had already moved from sleeping in the bedroom to sleeping in the front room after commenting that at least one of us should get a good night's sleep. This shows the kind of sacrificial man he was. He was concerned that his coughing and movement would have prevented me from sleeping.

When I walked in and saw Tyrone folded over the bathroom sink, it quickly dawned on me that this particular coughing episode was different. He exerted more force and the vomiting was near-continuous. I went in, caught him between breaths, held on to his body, rubbed his back and reassured him — as I had been doing — that he would be okay. I also stood with him and prayed over him.

The vomiting subsided and Tyrone spoke. "Babe, we need to go to the hospital right now," he said. "I am done going to different hospitals and GP surgeries to be told I'm okay and nothing is wrong with me. We're going and we're not leaving until they investigate and tell me what's wrong with me. This is not normal; I am not okay!"

We called an Uber and made our way to the Royal Free Hospital. When we arrived at A&E, we were asked to wait to see a triage nurse. When it was our turn, we went in and Tyrone explained how it had been for him physically. I shared how he had been over the last few months from my perspective. Up to that point, Tyrone had visited his GP's surgery, where his doctor told us that the symptoms were likely an indication of the return of his childhood asthma. He was prescribed an inhaler. They did, however, send him for an X-ray and shared with him that they did not find any abnormalities. He visited a number of A&E's but he was always sent home without medication and no further insight into what was going on with him.

The triage nurse at the Royal Free did a number of tests, one of which was a blood oxygen saturation test (measuring the amount of oxygen carried by your blood cells). When the results came back, the triage nurse was alarmed — Tyrone's blood oxygen was extremely low. He couldn't understand how Tyrone had got to that point, presenting with these symptoms while still being able to walk around and function to the extent he was. The triage nurse explained that Tyrone's results indicated that due to how fit and healthy he was, his body had been using its oxygen reserves. He immediately sent us through for Tyrone to receive emergency care, which included being placed on oxygen and an opportunity to receive further investigative tests, including another X-ray.

I remember that a consultant came into the room. He explained that he didn't usually work in that particular hospital however, he was brought in for a shift that day. We explained everything from the beginning. For once, Tyrone believed he was being heard by the consultant. After the

Chapter 5: Touched by an Angel

X-ray, the consultant explained that he had obtained and compared the results from the X-ray Tyrone had a couple of months prior, with the results from that day's X-ray. He asked us what we had been informed about the initial scan and we said that we had been told there were no significant findings.

He explained the following:
1. Both X-rays showed abnormal results. The white "cloud" (inside Tyrone's lungs, representing an infection) was initially present in the first scan and had increased.
2. Both X-ray results showed that Tyrone's left lung was partially deflated. Tyrone had been walking around with one-and-a-half lungs and we had no clue.

We were at a loss for words — well, I was. Tyrone fumed. Hot tears ran down his face because he had trusted the professionals from whom he had sought help. We felt like we had lost time. To know that he had been prescribed an inhaler when all of these things were going on was a disgusting slap in the face. The consultant apologised for the failings of the medical teams up to that point. He reassured us that he would do everything to ensure Tyrone received the correct care from that point onward. He reassured us that we were in safe hands and we really believed that he had been sent to help us — we had been touched by an angel.

CHAPTER 6:

My Worlds End

Tyrone didn't return home that night because they didn't know what was going on inside his body. As promised, our angel assured us that all necessary tests had been carried out. We were presented with three possibilities for Tyrone's symptoms, based on a number of factors:

1. Tuberculosis was the most plausible cause, especially due to the rapid onset and development of the symptoms, including his constant cough.
2. Sarcoidosis — I heard about it for the first time in the hospital. For those who are unaware, sarcoidosis is an inflammatory disease affecting multiple organs in the body. This was also a possibility due to the abnormal growth of inflammatory cells observed in Tyrone's lungs.
3. Cancer. This was presented as the least possible cause for his symptoms, mainly due to the fact that he was a healthy, strong twenty-eight-year-old with no history of sickness and no experience smoking or taking drugs. Another reason cancer was the least possible diagnosis was that his symptoms had gone from zero to ten in a very short time.

Based on the symptoms with which Tyrone presented and the test results (oxygen saturation and X-ray), the hospital decided to go down the TB route. He was immediately put in an isolation room and plugged into a huge oxygen machine. Only a limited number of people were able to visit him and those who did had to take precautions and wear a mask. It was overwhelming and scary for the both of us.

They moved Tyrone into a "normal" room once they'd ruled out TB. They tried their best to do a scan by putting a tube down Tyrone's throat but due to his constant coughing and having to be on oxygen continually, they decided that the safest option was to carry out a CT scan to observe what was going on in his lungs.

During the CT scan of his lungs, they confirmed that Tyrone's lungs were severely infected. At that moment, they made a surprising discovery: the scan picked up a small mass on his ribcage. They shared these findings with us and decided to perform a biopsy, right there and then.

I remember seeing it — it was so small. They said that although they doubted it was related to his symptoms, it was something substantial that might have been able to provide further information. Of course, our minds went directly to cancer.

Tyrone was discharged shortly with multiple portable tanks of oxygen and an oxygen machine to use at home shortly thereafter and we were instructed to wait for the results.

We headed to a nearby Starbucks, ordered and sat down with the aim to quietly process everything that had transpired over the past few days. We were relieved that Tyrone had finally received the proper support. The biggest surprise was, of course, the deflated lung and discovery of the mass on his ribcage. We drafted a text message to send to a few people, informing them of the news. We were told not to fear or worry, but to remain strong and trust God. We took the advice, finished our drinks, and headed home, returning to the hospital a week or so after being released.

The consultant brought us into the room and sat us down to share the biopsy results. The results showed that it was cancer. They didn't quite know which cancer it was, but they concluded that the mass on Tyrone's ribcage was directly linked to the infection in his lungs. Because they were unable to go into Tyrone's lungs to get a sample, they concluded that this was the probable cause. Tyrone was formally diagnosed with cancer.

Chapter 6: My World's End

Once again, he didn't return home.

I recall Tyrone and I sitting on the hospital bed shortly after receiving the news. Up to that point, I hadn't shed any tears in front of Tyrone, as he believed our tears to be an indication of a lack of faith. I was no longer able to hold my tears anymore. I started to cry.

My husband had just been diagnosed with cancer! The pain was unbearable. I didn't know what to do to help him; to help us. How the hell did we get here?

You see, losing Tyrone was my *greatest fear*. When we speak about fear, we all probably have one thing in mind that we hope will never happen. We may not mention it to anyone outside of the faint whisper in our hearts due to the probability of it actually happening being quite low. Instead, we do all we can to ensure the opposite occurs. The greatest fear in my whole entire life was losing my husband and the family God had newly given me as my own. My marriage to Tyrone represented so much for me and for us:

- We were finally married to someone we could call home, our mutual place of love, safety, strength and peace. Home wasn't in our four walls — my home was literally in Tyrone as my husband.
- We were both working on business plans, setting out short, medium and long-term goals and objectives.
- We planned to be wealthy, so we could build, enjoy and provide for our loved ones.
- We planned to move from London to Milton Keynes in 2016, where we would start trying for a family. We spoke about it all the time, even naming our two sons and two daughters. We recorded their names in our phones as a promise that it would happen. Tyrone came up with the name, Arayah, which he interpreted as "a ray of hope" and we agreed to give this name to our first daughter.
- We planned to travel the world as a family.

Tyrone was quite upset by my emotional state. He didn't understand why I cried when he needed me to be strong. At that point, we reached out to a very close friend of ours who explained to Tyrone the way I processed things and what it all meant from my perspective. I really thank God for you at that moment — thank you.

My personal writing in the following musings paints a picture of how I felt and my processing that night.

PERSONAL MUSINGS:

From Wedding Rings to Imperfect Dreams

At some point in our lives, we thought, dreamt, or even fantasized about meeting that "perfect person", having the "perfect wedding" and having the cutest "perfect family".

I remember searching online for my "perfect dress" long before I met my husband-to-be. Even before he proposed, I knew the style of ring that would look "perfect" on my pretty finger. I was ecstatic as I stood at the altar and he placed the "perfect ring" on my finger. Just like that, we were married!

I always knew that marriage was so much more than the "perfect" ring and wedding day, but it didn't stop me from waking up the following morning, thinking, *Snap! — I'm actually married!* Of course I was excited but honestly, I also felt really nervous. It was all very real and not in my imagination or my dreams, but in real life and in the eyes of God. I was actually accountable for someone else's life and I had to learn very quickly what it truly meant to be married.

We had beautiful, peaceful and fun times. In saying this, we also faced challenging times as you do in any other marriage. What I never expected was the surprise cancer diagnosis, one year and nine months in. That May evening, I just sat there and cried while the consultant calmly gave us the toxic news.

How could my fit, healthy, twenty-eight-year-old husband — who hardly ever got a headache — be diagnosed with cancer?

We hadn't even had the chance to enjoy our marriage properly yet!

We are Christians and we tithe!

How was it fair?

What about our perfect little family?

These were but a few of the trillion thoughts running through my overwhelmed mind. It was a huge mess and it was really hard. I was so tired and frightened. I felt so alone.

My heart had shattered. Our perfect future had been attacked. My dream of our perfect family was falling apart.

Amidst all of these feelings, I looked through my tear-stained eyes to see a man — my husband — who needed me now more than ever before. He needed me to hold him and reassure him that I was going to stay. He needed me to remind him that God's plans for us were good, even when it didn't seem like it. He needed me to keep hoping when he was too tired to do so. He needed to hear me say that I loved him and that his place as my king would always remain his.

As I sat there, Bible scripture 1 Corinthians 13 came to mind. I took hold of his hands, looked down at our wedding rings. I remembered our wedding vows and the commitment I made to him and the Lord. My ring wasn't as shiny as when it was first placed on my finger — it had a few scratches on it here and there, or maybe the tears had blurred my vision, but it definitely wasn't how I imagined it to be. *This* was *not* my perfect dream!

I sat on the hospital bed, faced with the reality of what my wedding ring symbolised:

SERVICE, HONOUR, PROTECTION, SELFLESSNESS, PATIENCE, HOPE, PERSEVERANCE, FAITH, TRUST, COMPASSION, FORGIVENESS, STRENGTH and PURPOSE!

So, I made the decision to stand next to him — to stand next to *us* — irrespective of how hard it got. I didn't know what tomorrow would bring, but I chose to trust *The One* who not only held it but created it.

It wasn't what I had imagined or hoped for, but I had no regrets. It was an honour and the best decision I never thought I'd have to make.

So, I ask you this — male, female, young, old, single, or married: what does a wedding ring mean to you?

CHAPTER 7:
The Hospital Room

Due to the severity of his symptoms and the rapid growth of the infection in such a short amount of time, the consultants decided they were unable to treat Tyrone at the Royal Free Hospital. At that point, they still hadn't identified which cancer it was and they were unable to do so with the specialists and resources they had. Tyrone stayed one more night in the hospital before he was transferred by an ambulance with flashing blue lights to University College London Hospital (UCLH), a hospital that specialises in young people with cancer.

We arrived at UCLH and were met by a team of specialists who were waiting for us. They transferred Tyrone to the specialist ward and explained who they were and why we were there. They explained that the biopsy results showed that Tyrone had a mass on his ribcage. Although there were no samples from his lungs, they had enough evidence to believe the mass on his ribcage was the primary cancer site and the lungs were actually filled with secondary cancer that had metastasized from the rib cage. Further analysis of the biopsy identified a rare form of cancer called a malignant peripheral nerve sheath tumour (MPNST) of the rib cage.

Moments after Tyrone was admitted, we were presented with information about the disease and the short, medium and long-term impact it was likely to have on both of our lives. We were requested to consider and make important life-changing decisions that had to be implemented immediately.

1. Chemotherapy — Due to the severity of Tyrone's symptoms, the hospital shared that the best course of treatment would be chemotherapy, but it had to commence immediately. We had little time to digest and process the decision, but we agreed.
2. Chemotherapy and its effect on fertility — Due to Tyrone's age, his health and the effect of chemotherapy, the hospital informed us of our options for having a family following treatment. This included Tyrone giving consent for me to use his semen if I wished to have his children if he died.

The discussions and considerations regarding the possibility of Tyrone becoming a father in the future and the processes he had to go through during this time, were incredibly painful for him to acknowledge, comprehend and process. It was not long ago that he had visualised holding his children in his arms and now only a few months later, he was being told that (1) there was the possibility that he may not be alive when his children are born and (2) if he lived, it was likely that he would not be able to conceive a child naturally with his wife.

The chemotherapy treatment affected him, as was stated in the textbooks. He glanced at the red liquid going into his arm and saw what he considered a poison.

His bad days saw the gradual loss of his hair, lethargy and difficulty smiling. His good days saw him laughing and cracking jokes with friends, doctors and nurses and encouraging the other patients on the ward. I am so grateful that I was present to see this so I could remember him that way. One constant with Tyrone was how he treated and honoured the people around him, even from his hospital room. He continued communicating with people with respect, no matter his frustration. His tone was always kind and he demonstrated so much love and continued to write and develop his business plans and ideas.

Chapter 7: The Hospital Room

While receiving chemotherapy, Tyrone spent time in and out of the hospital. I spent my time between the hospital, home and work. I continued to work, as unfortunately, I was not granted paid compassionate leave. My week was split sleeping at home in between the time spent with Tyrone at the hospital. I was my happiest when I was with him as we could be a true married couple, watching movies on his phone, laughing and dreaming of our future together. Like before, Tyrone slept upright and I slept on the bed next to him. What was different was that now he had access to specialist support.

God really did supply us with *helpmeets*. The nurses and doctors who were so kind to Tyrone and I. We organised visitors together so that Tyrone had ample time to rest and he wouldn't feel fatigued or overwhelmed. Tyrone and I were always so grateful, particularly for the following people below and we would like to say:

- Thank you to those of you who came to sit with Tyrone, especially when I wasn't able to be with him.
- Thank you to those of you who came to sit with both of us, becoming a shoulder on which I could rest my head and cry real tears outside of the hospital ward.
- Thank you to those of you who came to be with me at home.
- Thank you to those of you who continued to make him smile and who met him where he was and continued to dream with him.
- Thank you to those of you who reached out to me and Tyrone over the phone via text message, phone call, or social media.
- Thank you to those of you who prayed and interceded for us, privately and corporately.
- Thank you to those of you who carried out chores and activities for us.

- Thank you to those of you who brought food and provisions for Tyrone and I both to the hospital and to our home.
- Thank you to those of you who sowed monetary seeds during this season of our lives.

There are so many other categories of people I have not mentioned here, but I honour each and every beautiful seed, seen and unseen. Thank you from the very depths of my heart. I am eternally grateful.

CHAPTER 8:

We're Still Standing!

I personally don't want to lose you or the future we've dreamed about together, so I will boldly fight the good fight of faith so that we may see it together. — Tyrone Mitchell, 5th August 2015

My response:
Thank you, babe, for your words.
I don't want to lose you or our future either and I am looking forward to spending the rest of my life with you,
so I will continue believing that God will show himself in this situation.

We had no idea from where the cancer came or why it had entered our lives because, as I mentioned in previous chapters, Tyrone neither smoked nor used drugs. He did not really trust modern medicine and thus was not inclined to use over-the-counter medication, such as painkillers. He always lived a healthy lifestyle, participated in a range of sports from Taekwondo to running and he ate a well-balanced diet.

In spite of the confusion, considerations, questions, doubts and fears, we intentionally made a decision as husband and wife to believe that what was happening was nothing but a deep pit in the road and a short-term walk through the darkest of wildernesses. We decided that it would not be the end! Because of this, we continued to express our love any way we were able and were intentional in the way we honoured one another and our hopes for our future.

During this time, we communicated our desires for the full restoration of Tyrone's health and we asked people to pray for us and with us. A prayer call was set up by a dear pastor we both loved, which created the opportunity and provided a platform for our friends and loved ones to add their faith to ours in prayer, standing with us on the Word of God.

Even though Tyrone's medical team had remarked earlier that he seemed to be getting better, things took a turn when the first line of chemo was not completely effective in destroying the cancer cells.

Tyrone was given a second round of chemotherapy, presented as the last option available, due to the severity of the symptoms. Every time Tyrone and I expressed our faith in his healing and full recovery, the hospital staff reinforced that he would eventually die — they could not specify exactly how long he had left to live — and that we were about to enter the phase in his treatment plan where they would make him as comfortable as possible.

CHAPTER 9:

We Are Not Afraid of Death!

Tyrone completed the second round of chemotherapy, which did not have the impact we had all hoped. Hospital staff shared that, as this was the "last option" available to Tyrone, there was no other treatment they could give him and nothing else they could do for him.

We were at the darkest crossroad in our journey thus far. They weren't just saying that he was not responding to the current treatment or that there were still options he could try — they were stating, unequivocally, that there was nothing else they could do medically to treat him. I have tried to think back to how I actually felt at that stage, but I can't recall them and I'm glad, in a way. All I knew was that I felt incredibly low and disarmed.

A family friend put us into contact with private clinics with the hopes that Tyrone's case would be taken over by someone else. Maybe, if he had access to a different method of treatment or participated in a trial, things would end differently, but this approach proved unsuccessful.

Our hearts had been broken once more, and we had no idea to whom we could to turn for new information or to provide us with even a glimmer of hope. We were exhausted in so many ways. As husband and wife, there were ways we could relate and empathise with each other as individuals and ways we just couldn't.

Our two-year anniversary was approaching and we made a decision to celebrate with a trip to the countryside for a couple of days. This was one of the only moments in the past few months when Tyrone seemed at peace. We shared many moments of laughter as we reflected on our wedding day and the beautiful moments in our short two years together as a married couple. We used that time to re-ignite the spark in our hearts, re-establish our hopes for the future and affirm that we would remain strong.

Tyrone returned to the hospital, where he was asked to consider either staying in a hospice or returning home. Tyrone made the decision to return home, so we entered discussions with a patient discharge support worker to plan how that might work. Considerations included improving the current layout of our home and setting up specialised equipment to ensure that Tyrone was supported and remained as comfortable as possible.

On this part of our journey, Tyrone continued affirming his hope in the Word of God and he did his best to communicate encouragement and the steps we had to continue to take. Some of the words he shared with me are:

Step 1: Know what you want and find it in the "Word".

Step 2: Meditate on the Word so that it builds a picture of what you want.

Step 3: Take ownership of the Word by believing that you have received what is rightfully yours. To do this, you must affect a mentality of ownership.

Step 4: Praise God! Give Him thanks for all that He (God) has done.

PERSONAL MUSINGS:
Do You Believe That I Am a Good Father?

I've added these musings here because up until 30th September 2015, the day Tyrone died, we really believed that God was a good father. We believed this with all that was within us, so although I wrote the following many months after Tyrone's passing, I believe it fits perfectly here.

> *Do you believe I am a good father?*
> *Yes, I am your God, but do you believe*
> *I am a good father to you?*

At the time of writing this, I am in one of the most challenging seasons of my life. I cannot even write about it because it is just so hard and a part of me does not want to write about it because I am smack-bang in the middle of the fire. I am tired.

Truthfully speaking, last Sunday, after resting up from my performance as Ruth, the widow in *The Lighthouse Production*, I decided I was not going to write this month. I stated this on social media and posted a video of my performance instead. You see, the enemy heightened his attack the day before the production and I had to gather all of my emotions and strength just to get through it all. God had sent my fellow, beautiful, Lineage of Grace Ladies — the ladies who performed as Tamar, Rahab, Mary, and Bathsheba — to pray for me that day. Thank you, ladies! I was in tears, but in His grace and His strength, I delivered and His name was glorified.

About an hour ago, I woke up with my spirit singing the worship song: "That is why you are called Jehovah...what you said you would do, that is what you will do." I sang it automatically in my heart and I was comforted by this, but I didn't grasp the words and concepts of the song.

I heard the Holy Spirit ask the question, "Do you believe what you are singing?"

I answered yes and went on to sing, "You're a good, good father. It's who you are. I am loved by you. It's who I am."

Again, the Holy Spirit asked me, *Maria, do you believe I am a good, good father to you? Do you actually believe it right now, with everything you're going through?*

I listened to a sermon once, where the preacher stated that when you hear God say something twice, you had better listen. At that exact moment, I was reminded of the biblical story of God calling Samuel. I stopped singing, checked myself and asked myself the question, "Do I truly believe He is a good father? Do I currently believe He is a good father TO ME?" Besides being grateful for my good health and the gift of life, besides being grateful for my family and loved ones, besides being grateful for my work and having a home, for what was I grateful? What do I believe?

My heart visualised all of the things I'd believed God would bless me with, hopes of a dream home and my greatest hope of having a husband and a family. I visualised my children calling me mummy and running to me and this made me smile.

I decided to list all of the things for which I was currently grateful for outside of the "normal" list above and it struck me that I couldn't list anything — not one thing. I realised that I had been reciting this list automatically and not just to people but to myself. It was automatic because I have been stating what I think I should say and not what I actually believed.

Then, the Holy Spirit spoke to me clearly: "Maria, you are holding onto the right things. You are holding onto hope for the future, and this is good, *but* this is not enough to get you through! You have to hold onto the truth that *I am a good, good Father. It's who I am.* That doesn't change; it cannot change. What you are hoping for will change, but I will never change; I cannot change. You have to hold onto the truth that *I am and will always be your good Father.* You have to hold onto this *even more* than you hold onto that for which you hope for!"

It was at that very moment — just before I started writing this in the early hours of this morning — that it struck me: the reason my current trial had been even more challenging was because I had been holding onto hope (hopes, dreams, promises for my future) when I should be holding onto the truth that He is my good, good father.

My good father, whose thoughts towards me are always good. My good father who loves me. My good father, whose faithfulness endures outside my hopes and dreams for the future. My good father, whose promises of good is infallible because He cannot lie. My good father, who remains good regardless of what I go through. In my trial, in my pain, in my tears and in my anguish, He remains faithful.

This is where I need to place my hope! Sometimes, in seasons like this, holding onto my greatest hope — to have a family of my own — is not enough. Why? Because life can challenge even those things. Life can challenge their possibility. So the only reliable thing is the promise that God is a good, good father to me!

As mentioned, I had no intention of writing this, especially at 2 a.m. on a Saturday morning. I am physically tired, I don't feel so great and I couldn't care less about writing right now. I am being completely real with you here.

After my journey of walking with God, I am quickly — and at times, slowly and hard-headedly — learning to not just to listen and follow His instructions, but to discern the tone. I *had* to write this piece. I am not entirely sure why I had to write it; all that I know is that someone needs to read it.

CHAPTER 10:

My Final Stand

I sat to draft the following note, texting a copy to Tyrone, twenty-nine days before he had passed. I called this *My Final Stand*.

Overcoming my Fear of Death I believe that my husband will continue to live:

1. God has shown him what He wants him to accomplish on earth — this has not been accomplished yet.
2. I don't believe God would have allowed us to get married if it were His will for him to die.
3. We have been shown a future together, which includes bearing children and raising them together.
4. Tyrone has no desire to die; he wants to live to accomplish his purpose.

   With all of this in mind, I will not fear death itself.

   If we live, we live to the Lord; and if we die, we die to the Lord. So, whether we live or die, we belong to the Lord (Romans 14:8).

5. My husband's life does not belong to me; I do not hold his life in my hands.
6. Jesus loves him more than I do; his life is in God's hands. Though we believe that he will live, if he were to die, it will be God's will.
7. He will be in a safe place, reigning with Jesus and I will be with him again.

8. If death does come, I will continue to trust God and serve Him regardless; I had a predetermined purpose to fulfil before I met Tyrone. Though it will be painful, naturally speaking, God will equip me to go through it.

9. Jesus will always reign as my Lord and Saviour, and I will continue to trust Him and serve Him, come what may.

My decision: I choose to trust God, regardless of the outcome. I do not fear death and I let the fear go from my heart. I relinquish all things into God's hands, knowing that God's perfect will, will be accomplished in both of our lives forever. I am at peace that my husband's life is in God's hands.

CHAPTER 11:

Tyrone's Final Stand

Tyrone sent the following message to me on 25th August 2015, five days before he passed. He titled it his *"Daily Confession"*. He shared that these were God's words and promises, which he had personalised and he had decided to unequivocally stand on, irrespective of how he was feeling, the doctor's words and how things appeared.

He asked me to join him in *The Final Stand*:

For I, Tyrone, am not ashamed of the Gospel, for it is the power of God for salvation to everyone who believes, to the Jew first, and also to the Greek. For in it, the righteousness of God is revealed from faith for faith, as it is written, "The righteous shall live by faith." (Romans 1:16-17).

For faith is the assurance of things hoped for, the conviction of things not seen (Hebrews 11:1). *And without faith, it is impossible to please Him, for whoever would draw near to God must believe that He exists and that He rewards those who seek Him* (Hebrews 11:6).

Therefore I, Tyrone, can do all things through Him who strengthens me. (Philippians 4:13).

For He is able to do far more abundantly than all that I, Tyrone, can ask or think, according to His power at work within me. (Ephesians 3:20).

So I, Tyrone, humble myself under the mighty hand of God so that at the proper time, he may exalt me, casting all my anxieties on Him, because He cares for me. (1 Peter 5:6-7) *and will never leave me nor forsake me.* (Deuteronomy 31:6).

Maria and I stand firmly on God's Word for the manifestation of our new season in Christ, where the ashes of the last year become beauty.

CHAPTER 12:

Heavenly Graduation

And so, died the White Knight, now removed from the board, a sacrifice was not in vain as the Whites Kingdom begins to restore. For every white pawn that reaches the board's end trades in their pawn status, transformed into a new piece, "born again". — Tyrone Mitchell

It was in the early hours in the morning on Wednesday 30th September, when I received The Phone Call. I was informed that Tyrone had taken off his oxygen mask and refused to put it back on. I was placed on loudspeaker so Tyrone could hear me and I could hear him. Although muffled, I made out that Tyrone was adamant that he no longer wanted to wear the mask. I heard Tyrone share that he had been healed from his illness. I was kept informed with what was going on as I added other people to the call. In the space of a couple of minutes, Tyrone stood up from his hospital bed, lifted his arms to the sky, declared that he was healed and fell to the ground.

I won't go into detail about what was going on in my mind and the fear and dismay that gripped my heart violently. Even writing this is painful, as I can distinctly recall the sounds the moment it happened. Somehow, my heart remembers the emotions, physical tension and pain from that night. I will share the experience from my perspective, including my processing and steps.

I immediately called a friend of ours who also lived in North London and shared what had happened. He left his house and came to me. I also called another friend who lived close to the hospital, requesting he go immediately to the hospital to carry out CPR to resuscitate Tyrone. I gave him clear instructions: "They have stated that Tyrone is dead, but I don't believe it. Go to the hospital and perform CPR on him. I don't care what they say — I refuse to believe he is dead."

When our friend arrived at my home, I explained once again what had happened while on the phone. I was informed that Tyrone was dead however, I refused to believe it. We raced to the hospital and rushed up in the elevators. I remained silent the whole time. When I arrived at the room, it was quiet. There were no hospital staff around to greet me.

Tyrone lay on the bed. Even then, I refused to believe he had died. I was extremely upset with the hospital staff for not reapplying his oxygen mask. I demanded that it be reattached. They didn't understand my request and they tried to explain the reason why it had been taken off. So much was happening and it was just too much. We had a family friend — someone Tyrone looked up to — on one phone on loudspeaker and my pastor on another phone while we contacted family and friends. As the minutes passed, more calls came in and more people arrived.

We were all processing, crying, in shock, and experiencing every other emotion you could imagine. I've said this before, but I don't understand why my heart remembers not only the words but the emotions to this day. As I write this, I just want to stop because it's still painful.

The room started to fill with people — so many people — including family members, close friends, pastors and leaders. I distinctly remember a moment where I broke down. Thinking back, I believe this was the first time that day I actually acknowledged what had happened and I began to comprehend what had happened. I was sitting on a chair sofa next to the dear friend that had picked me up, the same dear friend who had walked closely with us every single step of our journey, the same friend that had been at the hospital only days before. He reached out to embrace me and I just wept on his knee. Everything came flooding out and I sobbed hard.

Many moments passed, I am sure. Another distinctive moment that I share any time I have the opportunity, or I am instructed by God to share my journey, is remembering standing in front of everyone as Tyrone's body lay on my left-hand side. There were so many faces in the room, so many hearts shattered. I have no idea why I opened my mouth to speak — it wasn't the "ideal" moment for it — but I uttered these words:

"My heart is broken, and there's so much pain. I don't know why this happened and I don't understand why this happened. I don't know why I'm saying these words and all of this does not make sense; however, irrespective of what has happened, I declare that God is still faithful."

I looked over at two of my pastors and requested the following: "Pastors, please always remind me of these words. Please, do not ever let me forget that God is faithful."

When I share the words I spoke that day, I always describe them not only as words but as heavenly inspired words spoken by the Holy Spirit through me. These were prophetic words, direct from the heart of God, spoken through my lips. I believe these words were Apostolic declarations I had spoken into the atmosphere, which went ahead and set me up for what was to come.

CHAPTER 13:

I Will Get Up!

Initially, I was unsure as to whether to write these words as a separate chapter and I had planned to fit it in as I continued writing about my journey. I finally decided to write it, as this was a significant and pivotal point for me immediately after Tyrone died.

Around a week after Tyrone's passing, I returned to my house and spent my first night there alone. I refer to it as my house as it definitely didn't feel like a home. Since Tyrone had left, it was no longer *our* home.

I went to bed one night and stayed in bed, weeping. I can't recall how long I was in bed — it could've been hours, a day, or more. To this day, I remember speaking to myself, saying the following words:

"I am not going to leave this bed. I won't leave to brush my teeth, bathe, or go to work. I am in too much pain to leave my home however, if I receive a phone call asking me to travel around the world to speak about my experiences, to tell my story, I would actually get up! I would get out of this bed, wipe my tears, and speak to God's people. I will get up and go!"

Purpose called out to me, and I answered.

When I share my story, I always mention the above quote, as I truly believe that, once again, just like in the hospital room, these were prophetic, life-activating words. In my shock, in my pain, in my brokenness, life, hope and purpose called out to me. God's purpose called out to me and I responded and held onto Him with the little hope I had left. Purpose's call and my response became my only stable anchor.

I have to mention this here. Before I met Tyrone, I knew I had been called to serve and support others. I knew I had been called to bring people together. I knew that I was going to share my story — about my life as I had gone through so much prior to meeting Tyrone that I could not envisage it getting any harder — with the world.

Not only was I *aware* of my purpose, but I was "walking in it" by supporting people in my capacity as an education practitioner, working in the youth and young adult ministries at church, volunteering with young people and creating opportunities for people to come together in fellowship. I always knew I had a pastor's heart with prophetic gifting and I knew I had been called to the mountains of education and family (spheres of influence).

I really believe that because I was already aware and activated in the remit of purpose, my spirit was able to speak out and go forth when I was met with death (in every sense of the word). I believe that, due to my experience walking with God, I was able to declare Him faithful. To be honest, I don't believe that I comprehended or believed the crucial words and declarations I spoke on the day Tyrone died, nor the words I expressed as I lay on my bed. I can now say that, back then, I didn't really understand God's faithfulness. Like I mentioned in an earlier chapter, I didn't really understand what I was requesting when I asked God to "Make my heart like David's after His."

Since (1) I hadn't planned to say it (declaring God faithful and speaking my willingness to share God's faithfulness with the world); (2) I definitely hadn't felt (emotionally) as if it were true; (3) I had no emotional, mental, or physical desire to go; and (4) I saw no evidence of God's faithfulness (I was literally face-to-face with death and it looked like God had ignored all of our petitions and promises to keep Tyrone alive, heal him and grant us a wonderful future together); it must have been something — someone — in me that spoke out. It could only have been the Holy Spirit once again.

CHAPTER 14:
The Audacity of Life

*"Either way, it's none of my business what you choose to do,"
says Grandfather Clock. "I'll just keep greeting the passing of
time, twenty-four hours a day, seven days a week,
non-stop."* — Tyrone Mitchell

I remember waking up and looking out of my front room window. The streets looked the same. Traffic buzzed past and people chatted happily with their friends. How dare they carry on like everything was normal? How dare life continue as usual, as if it hadn't happened, as if Tyrone hadn't existed? How could things just continue as usual?

It was like the earth had just wiped Tyrone from existence. Yes, I had proof that he had been here and we had been married, but everything else just continued on. I still received dumb emails in my inbox and stupid phone calls. What upset me about this part of the journey was that although our friends and loved ones were grieving, I felt as if they were still able to carry on with their lives and I hated that.

I remember leaving my home to go to the shops. I felt really insecure — even dirty — as I walked the streets. I felt as if people could see and sense what had just happened as if there were a disgusting stench of some sort about me. I remember looking up and making eye contact with someone, then quickly directed my gaze to the floor. Although I didn't share these feelings and experiences with people, it took me a long time to process it all.

I stayed away from church for a while. When I did return to church, I sat at the back of the balcony so people wouldn't see me and I would be able to leave church swiftly and with minimal interaction with people. In environments such as at church, I received many uncomfortable glances, stares and the sorrowful looks. I felt like people were standing on the corner, talking about what had happened. I hated it when people came up to me and said, "I'm sorry for your loss." I actually hated the use of the word "sorry" as a form of condolence because I couldn't understand why people were sorry. I wanted to ask them why they were apologising.

I remember a dear friend of Tyrone's and mine, posting a message on Facebook. He wrote his status as if he were "communicating" to Tyrone. It made me angry because I didn't understand why he would speak to Tyrone as if he were still here. Tyrone wasn't here anymore, so why would he speak to him and why did he have to put it on Facebook? I even remember texting him to explain that I was upset by his post.

I'm so grateful for the people who sent food parcels, those who prayed with and for me and those who sowed into me financially in this season. I'm also grateful for the prayers and people who said sorry when they didn't have the right words to say — I understand the weight of it now.

PERSONAL MUSINGS:

My Love has Nowhere to Go

Our relationship was a whirlwind; some would say it was a fairy tale. We were friends, talking, hanging out and getting to know each other. Feelings developed and we decided to give loving each other a go.

Love developed...

We dated with the intention of marriage. He was in my heart and on my mind all the time, and I was on his. We learned to care for each other's feelings and cater to each other's needs. We learned about each other's characters, habits, hopes, dreams, insecurities and fears.

Love grew...

I married a man who truly loved me, not just my somewhat attractive sides, but every side of me. He loved my hidden sides, those that were not visible to the world. He demonstrated his love daily, through his embrace, his mesmerising smile, his discipline, his unfailing trust, his belief in me and his unrelenting faith in God. He provided me with security and comfort and loved me by being an exemplary leader and role model in our home.

Love poured...

It was easy to love him. He made it easy by being kind, patient and affectionate towards me. I know it may seem a little clichéd, but I loved him with my whole being. It wasn't that butterflies-in-my-stomach-infatuation-singing-in-the-rain kind of love that the world acknowledges as *love*, *but* the kind of love that can only be compared to the unconditional way God loves us. It took time and patience to develop and grow into the beauty it was — an enriching, intense, consistent, selfless and pure kind of love. I learned to show him love in times of celebration, in times of challenge and in our season of hell. A love like that has no depth and I was ready to love him like that for all of eternity.

Love poured out.

So, when Tyrone went to be with his Father, it was as if the supply of my love poured out had violently stopped and had nowhere to go. I was no longer able to pour my love into my husband. I was no longer able to receive his comfort and affection. The possibility of creating new memories was cut off. All of our hopes for the future and having a family together had been cut off. No longer did I have a husband into who I could pour my love, celebrate life and dream with. No longer did I have a husband to tell me he was proud of me. My love had been cut off and violently so. My life had drastically halted. My love had nowhere to go!

People may have assumed that the only loss I'd experienced was Tyrone leaving me, but it really wasn't. Everything had changed! I had to cling onto Jesus for dear life as He put the pieces of my heart back together. As I walked through the dark valley of grief, I had to try really hard to keep sight of His light. I had to remain teachable, even when I really didn't want to. The label of being a widow had been thrust upon me. Life had challenged me to start again and I had to learn to dream new dreams. With my tear-stricken face, I had to look consciously to God as He revealed the re-calculated route of my life.

On my way to work this morning, the memory of Tyrone's morning kisses came to mind, gripping my heart with so much pain, but I had two choices: to smile or cry. I chose the former. To say it's been hard is an understatement, but I'm still standing and most importantly, I'm still walking forwards. Though my love has nowhere to go, I will, nevertheless, always have a Heavenly Father who is always ready to receive and demonstrate His love for me.

CHAPTER 15:

Time, Death and Love — My Nemesis

Watching the film *Collateral Beauty*, starring Will Smith, for the second time recently, reminded me of how I perceive the three elements of life: Love, Time, and Death. In the movie, Will Smith's character seeks answers from the universe by writing letters to Love, Time and Death, following the death of his daughter.

Before I watched the movie, I recall actually comprehending and interacting with all three of these elements. I personally remember hating everything about Time, being disquieted by Death, and falling out of love with Love.

I recall comprehending and relating to Time first. As I shared in the previous chapter, there were many days spent at home, standing by the window after Tyrone passed. I noticed how the birds squeaked as they flew by, the sun continued to shine, children played happily with their friends and cars drove past. I was angry because I felt as if it was a slap in my face every time I had to go to sleep because it was dark outside. I was angry because I was expected to wake up and carve out my day without having any control. I hated that Time just carried on.

The clock continued to tick, irrespective of how I felt that day and the days seemed to have forgotten that Tyrone had actually existed. It was like the universe — the world — had spat him out and erased him from all of existence. Because of how much he had meant to those that loved him, the world should have stood still, or at the very least, something should have shifted with the physical proof, like the soundtrack of *The Hunger Games* ringing out each time someone died in the film. I honestly expected something like this to happen. I hated that the people who loved Tyrone carried on, went to work and had the luxury of going back home to their husbands, wives and children. Church services continued as normal, and people celebrated birthdays, anniversaries and new births, and I was left with nothing.

I was disquieted by Death. The word, *disquieted*, means to "take away the peace or tranquillity, deprive of calmness or peace, disturb and make uneasy". In my journey after Tyrone passed, Death was the person who had robbed me of my beloved husband. Now that he was gone, I really did not have any say. I saw Death as someone who had taken everything that represented peace, joy and the hope of a future with Tyrone. Because it was finite, I felt silenced by Death and what it represented. Because I felt silenced by it, I did not focus on it because in the initial days, Death had won as far as I was concerned.

The interaction with Love was interesting because I really wanted to be angry and hate Love. I felt let down by Love in a major way. I was someone who had lived my life doing my best to treat people really well and love them. I was intentional when it came to Love, believing I was hard-wired for commitment. Out of Faith, Hope and Love, I believed Love as the greatest of the three, had a responsibility to protect and honour me.

What is interesting is that, as I look back, it was *Love* that appeared first. It was Love that had motivated me to marry Tyrone and it was Love that compelled me to love him when he was ill. Love kept my mind intact. Love declared God's faithfulness in Tyrone's hospital room.

Love spoke out when I responded to the call to get up to speak around the world a few days after Tyrone had passed because God knew I had no emotional or physical interest to do so. It was Love that comforted me when I cried in the days, weeks and months after Tyrone had died and it is still Love that hopes I will find love in the arms of someone else. It is the same Love that was in the beginning and is present now.

Love gave me the will and strength to hold onto my mind when the enemy wanted to rip it from me and Love clung to me when I told Him to go away. When I ignored, resented, and lost my belief in Love, it clung to me, whispering to me that I was precious, I was beautiful, and that I, Maria, still had everything to live for, besides Tyrone. The *person* of Love became my only reliable anchor, the only one of the three that's not compassionless like Time and callous like Death. To me, Love was and continues to be patient, kind, protective, trusting, and hopeful. Contrary to popular belief, it was not Time but Love that persevered and healed.

Love really did not fail.

PERSONAL MUSINGS:

Into my Daddy's Arms

I'm on my sofa this Sunday evening, with tears running down my cheeks. These are not tears of sadness but of overwhelming love and admiration for God. I've been reflecting on the season I'm in and the recent challenges I have experienced — challenges that have brought me to the end of myself.

This month has been the hardest since Tyrone has passed. I never, ever believed it could get any harder. I can't begin to articulate what I've experienced. I can't erase that Monday morning out of my mind. I remember telling a friend that survival was more important than purpose. Those who know me know that I would not ordinarily say anything like that, but I have said it because it was just too much for me at the time. My dear friend, thank you for being present, correcting and challenging me with the truth, even when I didn't want to hear it.

I'm here because just like Shadrach, Meshach and Abednego's experiences, I had someone — *The One* — standing beside me in the fire.

I have been scared, I have been frustrated and I have been tired. My flesh wanted to give up, but my soul wouldn't allow it. This season has been particularly arduous because in spite of how I have felt amidst the chaos, I have had to rise up, force my spirit to be quiet and come to a place of peace.

After getting off the phone from those whom God has used to speak life into me, I was faced with life's reality. Things become real when you're by yourself. I've had to spend more time feeding on the Word. I've had to be intentional with how I spend my time, basking in God's presence every opportunity I get. I've had to intentionally spend more time in prayer seeking God. I've had to cry out and hold onto him when every single thing seemed as if it were crumbling around me.

I haven't had the luxury of waking up to see what the day brings. Naturally speaking, life and its circumstances doesn't make sense. I've had to affect a change, command my day and subject my spirit, emotions and body to the Word of God. I've had to speak out God's Words when others speak fear and destruction. For the first time, I have been "forced" to trust Him with my life.

Just a month ago, I wrote about my love and that my overflow of love had nowhere to go. I never expected that a couple of weeks later, I would enter a new season in which I would be challenged to discover God's love for me when all else failed.

In my new season of quietness, I am starting to discover the height, width, depth and vastness of God's love for me. I am discovering just how committed the Holy Spirit is to keeping me focused on Jesus and his purpose for my existence. He is incredible and consistent. He is my cheerleader, continuously speaking words of the affirmation my soul desires. I am learning that God's love can reach deep down into the darkest of pits and it has the power to pull me out.

I am learning that I am not alone, I was never was alone and I never will be alone. I am learning that the season I'm in is good. Yes, I am in the best place! I think there's something quite unique when you meet with God at your end and you're empty, unclothed and have nothing to lose.

I've always known that Jesus loves me. I've read about it, I've been taught about it and I've spoken about it. He has demonstrated his love for me over and over again; however, for the first time, I am learning about another dimension of God, that of a Father, My Daddy, who really loves and cares for his daughter, a daughter who has had her life, love and dreams pulled out from under her feet. I lost a best friend in Tyrone, but I gained a new one who was always there, waiting for me to find him. For the first time, I'm discovering that there is nowhere too dark, too sorrowful or too overwhelming that My Daddy's love can't penetrate. With His arms outstretched, He is waiting for you, too.

As I continue to walk along this new path, I am learning that His love brings peace. It brings clarity. It brings strength. It brings hope. It doesn't matter how rough the sea gets because I have an infallible anchor. Every day, I learn to trust *this* anchor more. I believe the storm(s) is an indication of how great my purpose is. I hold on to his promises even tighter now because I am learning to trust that my Father desires the best for me. I have discovered that my love now has somewhere to go — straight into My Daddy's arms.

CHAPTER 16:

I Am Not a Widow!

Maybe it's the stigma surrounding the word, but I grew up believing that becoming a "widow" was one of the most unfortunate and negative experiences a woman could ever go through. As I never knew any "widows" growing up, I pictured them as older women who had lost their husbands due to old age or illness. I perceived them as unattractive, not based on their physical appearance but based on the unfortunate circumstance in which they found themselves. I perceived them as timid and silenced by a dark cloak of death and loss. As an adult, it wasn't a term or status that crossed my path often. I personally didn't know any, so as they say, out of sight, out of mind.

I've intentionally put the status "widow" in quotation marks. Since this status was handed to me — actually, more like being shoved into my face — I've had to fight not to let "it" overpower me and define *who I am*. Yes, it is true that my husband has passed. Yes, it is true my ring finger is currently naked. Yes, it is true that, at times, I experience intense waves of loneliness; however, I refuse to let my current natural circumstances define who I see when I look in the mirror or how I act or how I am portrayed.

Firstly, I have already destroyed my initial ideology, that a "widow" is someone who is old, unattractive, timid and silent. My experiences have made me even more beautiful. I am more beautiful now because of the strength I carry. I am more courageous now as I continue to discover the authority I have in Jesus Christ. I refuse to be silenced as I use my life experiences to have an impact on others and empower them. The people I've met who are or have been on the bereavement journey are some of the most inspirational and powerful people I have ever come across.

Secondly, I have made the concrete decision not to let it define how I think, the words I use, and the actions I take. Life consistently questions who I am:

"Were God's promises true for you or did you imagine them? What about the stigma that's been attached to you? What do you have to show for being married? You are in your thirties, and you don't have any children, not even one! Who will want to marry a "widow"? What hope do you have for the future?"

My environment consistently questions who I am. At times, I deal with uncomfortable looks from people when they see me. I have to respond to the questions such as "how are you coping?" when I see myself "living". Even after notifying businesses of my husband's death, I still receive mail referring to me as "Mrs.", an insensitive reminder of the sacred union of which I used to be a part. It hurts that people still keep their distance from me through their lack of contact and communication. Daily, I am reminded that the two that had become one are officially one again. It was an outcome that was not due to infidelity or indifference, nor was it one requiring or requesting my consent.

Regardless of this, I wake up, I get up, brush away my tears when I need to and keep it moving. I am not ashamed to be a woman who no longer has her husband. I married the best man I know. I gracefully and relentlessly fulfilled my duty as an honourable wife and I know I gave all of me, right to the very end. I just refuse to be shackled by this and I refuse for the "facts" of life to have the loudest voice. Why? Because there is no other option for me.

I choose to see my battle scars as a memorial of God's grace and faithfulness rather than the enemy's trail of desolation and destitution. I have to keep believing. I have

Chapter 16: I Am Not a Widow!

to keep moving forward. I have to hold onto the truth that my God is faithful, that everything will work itself out and that *all* things — every single thing — is working out for my good. Yes, these are my experiences. Yes, they remain a massive part of my life and have contributed to shaping who I am. It is *not*, however, my identity; it is not my end. Widowhood is just a prominent chapter in a beautiful story that continues to unfold. It is just the beginning for me.

CHAPTER 17:
I Have Concluded that God is Still Faithful

> *"My heart is broken, and there's so much pain. I don't know why this happened, and I don't understand why this has happened. I don't know why I am saying these words and all of this does not make sense. Irrespective of what has happened, I declare that God is still faithful. Pastors, please always remind me of these words. Please do not ever let me forget that God is faithful."* — Maria Mitchell, Wednesday, 30th September 2015

At that moment in the afternoon on 30th September, I certainly did not "see" that God was faithful — there was no "natural evidence" of this. I did not "feel" that God was faithful — we stood on God's promises and interceded daily, yet Tyrone still died. I didn't understand anything that was going on. I was numb and completely empty, but something deep down inside refused to give up on life. My whole being was overwhelmed and had reached the breaking point, so I went into "automatic". I had never planned for those words to come out, but they did. Even in the face of death, I declared God's faithfulness and His sovereignty.

God is faithful. If you have ever read my social media posts or have met and had a conversation with me, you would know that I live by these three words. They are the same words I shared in Chapter 12 and the words above are the ones I spoke out when Tyrone died. I'm not sure if I believed the words I said that day, but I do know that I did not comprehend them, nor did I realise how much they would shape my journey. However, these three words have meant everything to me, anchoring me and literally saving my mind, heart and life.

God is Faithful has become my life's motto. It has become the very foundation of who I am, my peace and my hope. My sound mind stems from and clings to God being a faithful.

Shortly after Tyrone died, God spoke to me to tell me that I won't lack for anything and everything I touch will be blessed. One area of my life in which God has promised this blessing is in the area of finance. He specifically promised that I would be wealthy when it came to finances, especially now that my husband — the head of my home and my covering — has gone. God promised that He Himself would take care of me. I took hold of His promises and have held on to them ever since.

Following these promises and my experience losing Tyrone, I thought that life would become easier; however, this has not been the case. It has been immensely challenging, mentally, emotionally, spiritually and relationally. There have been days when life has challenged my existence: *"Who Am I?" "Why Am I like this?" "What am I doing here?" "Why do I think these thoughts and act this way?"* There have been quite a few things, behaviours, past experiences, and memories (good and bad) which have surfaced, darkness from way back in my childhood.

As I embarked on the desolate journey of "widowhood" I really expected to see and experience the more endearing and comforting side of God in my journey — you know, God as my Father and me as His daughter. I expected God to keep negative experiences away and let me experience only the good He had in store for me. I did not expect to experience days that would bring me to tears and I definitely did not expect that my heart would be broken again. I did not expect the challenge of my mental and emotional health to be so intense. I did not expect to deal with feelings of inadequacy and worthlessness at the depth I did. I didn't believe I could ever attend church and experience feelings of depression and thoughts of suicide months on. I didn't expect this to be my new journey — I really didn't.

I'll share this with you — only a few of you know of the season in which I experienced one of the greatest heartbreaks of my life. I experienced everything from feeling used, dishonoured, abandoned, scared, exhausted, hopeless and felt depression coming on once again. I would describe this as rock bottom for me — a place I never ever would have imagined being again.

I remember weeping in bed one night and I said to God, "I can't go through this pain any longer. I am going to sleep now. When I go to sleep, I expect one of two things to happen: (1) I do not wake up and I find myself in heaven, or (2) I wake up on Earth in this room, open my eyes and see you sitting opposite me. I literally believed that one of these two things would happen. It had to happen because of everything coursing through my heart, mind and soul. I honestly didn't expect to wake up on this Earth by myself.

The following morning, I opened my eyes and realised that I was in my body. I looked ahead, and God was not there. I was disappointed because it meant that it was not yet my time to be in heaven. The feeling of agony and despair rushed in, but they were blocked by words of love: "My beloved daughter, I am not here in my physical form however, I *am* here in your heart. I have not left you, even in the place you are in now. It does not make sense, once again, but I have never left you. Please trust me to hold your hand as we walk forward. If the death of your husband could not break you, please do not allow this to break you. Please know that you are loved so dearly with a consistent love. I was your constant love back then and I will be, now and forever. Please trust that I am still a good and faithful Father to you."

So, I wiped the tears streaming down my face and decided not to run away but to cleave to the voice of God. I chose to take one step at a time and embark on my journey of self-love and healing from my deep pain and trauma. I can now say that this experience shaped who I am today and I am so grateful because it forced me to really listen, become sensitive to my needs, be still and quiet my spirit enough to sit with me, past and present. I forced myself to seek help and support as I learned to listen to and trust my inner-voice of love and set out to live within healthier boundaries and I am a better woman because of it.

As I declared His faithfulness at the beginning of my journey of "widowhood", God has held me accountable to my words and He has used my life as a tool to test my faithfulness to Him and demonstrate his compassion and grace towards others through me. Immediately after Tyrone died, God gave me a few clear instructions to follow, one being that I should demonstrate Christ's love, regardless of how I am perceived and treated. Another was to be consistent in how I communicate in love with those around me.

People who are aware of my entire story always ask how I have been able to love those who have not shown me love, and how I can be so consistent in every season. Even when I experienced heartbreak, when my heart was taken advantage of and was not honoured, or when I had been hurt, treated unfairly, when my efforts have been overlooked, somehow, I, Maria, have demonstrated the ability to remain consistent. This comes at a cost, the likes of which I have no words to articulate. One thing I can say is that no one can ever question two things about me: my ability to demonstrate love in and out of seasons and the grace in which I walk and demonstrate to those around me.

In every destructive and messed-up season into which I have transitioned — even those times I literally believed my normal mind was leaving me — I have heard my spirit

Chapter 17: I Have Concluded that God is Still Faithful

spring up to remind me of those words on 30th September 2019: "But Maria, didn't you declare God faithful? Hasn't He been faithful? Look how far He's brought you! Look at how resilient you are now. Look at how quickly you forgive now. Look at how deeply you're able to love now. Look at how different you process your thoughts and emotions now. Look at how He's using you to bring healing, hope and restoration to those around you. Isn't this evidence of his faithfulness? Yes, you don't know or understand the what's and whys of your seasons, but have I ever left you?"

Today, I can honestly say that I feel like my declaration on the day Tyrone died and my declarations in the days following his death set me up for what was to come, even to this very day. Before it got better, it really did get worse, but these prophetic words went ahead of me to contend on my behalf.

So, I write to say this:

God's faithfulness, at times, isn't initially seen on the worst days. There have been countless days when I have not felt like He is faithful and I didn't see His faithfulness, but I intentionally believed that He was, in spite of what was staring back at me. I made this decision quickly because I knew that the enemy was unleashing a vicious attack, not on my family, not on my hopes and dreams, but on my faith — he wanted my faith!

As I have experienced turbulent days, months, years and seasons on my journey, I know and trust that if Tyrone's death could not and did not destroy me — my heart and mind, my ability to hope and my capacity to love — then nothing on this Earth I have experienced, am still experiencing, or will ever experience can ever break or destroy me. Death in any and all of its forms has forever lost its hold on me; it cannot win!

By declaring God's sovereignty and faithfulness, I use God's faithfulness; His promises as my seeds, my deposits and my hope. I hold onto the fact that He is and can only be good, or he fails to be God. This seed has been and will continue to be my anchor, yesterday, today, and forever.

Are you waiting to feel, see, or understand? Like me, you may never have the privilege of ever understanding why something has happened. Had my intercessory prayers and those of Tyrone, our pastors and loved ones been in vain? Was healing real? Would I ever experience true love again? Was God really a Good Father?

What would your response be to these questions? In the situations and experiences I have intrinsically shared, would you still aver that God faithful? Is He really deep down in the depths of your heart and in the vastness of your mind? Off social media or in front of friends and family, would you still declare Him as faithful? Not on a Sunday, when you have on your "church face", but deep down in the closet of your heart and mind, is He really faithful?

CHAPTER 18:
A Widow's Call

I hadn't planned to write this chapter; however, as I was writing the previous chapter, I decided to add it in. I will keep it as brief as possible as there is much literature supporting the bereaved. I aim to share advice, suggestions, and a call to action as a young widow in the UK to people and groups in the community. All sections, points, considerations, and requests have been written from my own perspective and personal experience as I walk my journey.

To the Family of the Widow

I will keep this simple. You probably won't understand the intricate journey of your widowed daughter/sister/mother/aunt/niece/cousin however, you are one of the safest spaces for her. I know it breaks your heart, especially if you loved and had a relationship with her spouse, and I know it breaks your heart, having to watch a part of her die and other parts of her break down. You will be there when she takes a new breath alone, bravely taking a new step every day. We are eternally grateful for your consistent love. Might I kindly request a couple of things from you on her behalf?

- Please allow *her* to speak about *him* boldly and please support her when she acknowledges and celebrates him, even if it doesn't make sense to you. You may feel like this is doing more harm than good, but it is likely to help her heal. She shares in your presence because she trusts you with her greatest pains, disappointments, memories, hopes and desires. Honour her with the words with which you choose to respond and how you choose to respond.

- Please continue to hope on her behalf. Please hope from a place of compassion, patience and empathy. Might I also request that, as her family, you do your best to check in on her, especially on the anniversary of his death? This will mean more to her heart than you can imagine.

To the Friends and Loved Ones of the Widow

I never planned to write this section today, on 11th September 2019 but I need to. I found out earlier in the day that a young pastor in America died by suicide a couple of days ago. He was married with two young children. I took the news hard for reasons I understand and reasons I do not yet understand. I am heartbroken for his wife, his two sons and the friends and family he left behind. My heart goes out to the church community grieving his loss. I write this section from my own perspective and based on my personal experiences. I write this section on behalf of the widows (and widowers) across the world. As a voice and advocate for widows, I write to those closest to her and her beloved husband, who is no longer here. I have written a number of points below, which I kindly ask you to consider on her behalf. These points have been gathered and listed in order, based on a possible timeline of events that may occur.

1. **Acknowledgement**

    When you are made aware of an illness perceived as terminal, acknowledge that it is happening and reach out to the couple. I decided to list this first because I have spoken to many people in both of our lives, even those closest to us, who made the decision not to contact or reach out to us and "went missing" for the season. Although I was preoccupied with what was happening, Tyrone and I had discussions about this. Tyrone wanted people, especially those closest to us, to contact him.

2. Words and Questions

I know there are many thoughts that cross your mind when news of an illness or terminal diagnosis is received. Questions like, *What do I say? How do I say it? What if what I intend to say does not come out the way I want?* I ask you to not put pressure on yourself. An individual in this position is unlikely to be looking for you to have the answers. You won't ever have the *right* words. She does not expect you to say the right things at the right time.

People may not be as specific as me, but I did not do too well with the words, "I'm sorry for your loss," because something inside of me automatically responded with "It's okay" upon hearing these words when it definitely was not and would never be okay. Very early in my journey, I walked away after hearing these words thinking that there was no need for them to use the word "sorry" because it wasn't their fault. We will, unfortunately, come across people who have received news of an illness or terminal diagnosis, and we may be grieving someone close to us. In these moments, let's all be more intentional and creative with the words we choose to offer to express our condolences, thoughts and love.

3. Methods of Communication

Where possible, communicate via phone call rather than text, as your heart's intention through scribed words may be misread or misinterpreted.

4. Real Community

Being a friend doesn't mean you have to know what to do, nor is it a requirement or expectation that you will fix anything. Being a friend means sitting there with her in the hospital room, home and anywhere else she finds herself. Be present enough to feel her pain and be okay with her not being okay. Finally, in the words of Daniel Brooker (a widower who is now remarried), "Don't tell someone it's going to be okay, stay with them until they can say it."

To me, a real community shows up by providing groceries and meals or by supporting financially if the need is there. Open up your home to her so she can find respite away from the daily reminder of her four walls. Offer to help with contacting companies to inform them of the loss. Sleep over and watch a movie with her. Help to pack up her home when it's time for her to relocate from the marital residence.

Dear friends and loved ones of the widow, please know that you are in such a precious position. You are part of a group of people on which she is likely to lean for more consistent love, fellowship and comfort. You are part of a group of people who will emulate some sort of normalcy to her and for her. She will look to you for your consistency in your words paralleled by your actions.

Dear friends and loved ones of the widow, please take her in as one of your own. Please cover her and stand strong on her behalf. Please attempt to view her process through her eyes. It's okay if you do not understand as you never will. Please be present and walk with her at her pace as she learns to trust and entrust again.

A New Romantic Interest or Partner

- **Heal and develop yourself first**

    Ensure you have done or are doing the emotional work, healing and development in yourself before embarking on a romantic relationship with a widow.

- **Be intentional and clear in your mind:** Be clear about the reason you communicate with her

A widow may be in a position in which she can feel love and pain even deeper than when her husband was alive. She is extremely vulnerable and may desire a transaction for which you are not in a position to grant or you cannot make. Please back up your words with consistent actions and use this time as a gift, treating her with the greatest love and honour. Finally, choose to show up, rather than run away. Choose to listen more. Choose to seek understanding rather than be dismissive. Choose to apologise rather than defend. Choose to be a reflection of love and grace rather than give in to fear. These choices will bring much healing, hope, empowerment and restoration for both of you.

- **Have boundaries on your behalf as well as hers**

  This is not a time to say that you do not desire a relationship with her while choosing to be intimate at the same time. She is a woman who has been bereaved of the love of her life and her safe place in which she was encouraged and empowered to be emotionally and physically free. If you seek to cultivate a friendship, choose to practice boundaries with the words you say, how you say them and why you say them. Be considerate of how you choose to relate to her with your behaviour and actions.

- **Take your mutual intentions into consideration**

  When communicating, ensure boundaries are enforced when it comes to the amount of time and frequency of communication. There is so much I could note here, but as a widow, she is looking for the people in her life — especially someone she may have expressed a romantic interest in — to show compassion and care. Her heart may yearn to love quicker, deeper and more intensely now. Your boundaries will help contribute to her sense of safety.

- **Be patient and communicate openly with her**

    She will not communicate using her language, actions and behaviours like other women you know or have met because she is not like them. This is a journey on which she never chose to embark and if she is anything like me, she has to make a conscious, intentional decision and effort every day to "set" her will, attitudes and emotions through the lens of her beliefs, thoughts, reasoning and journey of grief, among other things. Making the decision to live meant that I had decided to stay alive in all of this while facing it head-on.

- **Make the effort to understand her**

    The majority of people I meet will never be aware of my daily processing, and only a handful of people will be trusted with it. For a widow to show interest in you after all of this has happened and is still happening, means she has decided to trust you with a part of her heart. Please, be patient with her, mentally, emotionally and physically. Allow her the space and freedom to navigate and express what she discovers to be *her* new normal. Build a friendship and relationship in which you are able to ask questions as she allows about her past relationship, her current place and her hopes of the future.

- **Select your words with caution and wisdom**

    This is true especially when the words are coming from a place of temporary frustration, insecurity or anger. As a woman whose primary language of love language is words of affirmation, I believe and agree with Dr. Albert Mehrabian's (1972) findings that a speaker's words form a fraction of his efforts. I observe the *tone* and *pitch* of an individual's voice, as well as the *speed* and *rhythm* of the words spoken. I also the observe *body language* and expression of communication. Since Tyrone has passed, one thing I have come to discover is that words (or the lack thereof) play a prominent role in how my heart is built or torn down. A widow processes a lot of words in her mind, some of which are her own and some that are not and she uses her strength to stay in a positive place. Your words — both positive and negative — can have an impact on a woman that can be expected or measured, whereas the same words expressed to a widow are likely to penetrate to deeper depths or cut on a grander scale.

- **Finally, allow the space in her heart for the husband she lost**

In an interview with a friend, I remember being asked how I planned to make room for a new love and relationship in my heart. I shared my explicit answer then and I will share it here. I don't plan to forget Tyrone. This means that the love we had and the journey we shared (the good, the bad, and the ugly) will always be acknowledged and celebrated. I shared that the children I will birth in my new chapter will know that 'Mummy had once married a man named Tyrone, whom she loved'. 'Sadly, he died, and Mummy embarked on a long journey of great pain, but also of beauty and purpose'. 'In this new season, she met Daddy, whom she loves very much. From this love, they gave birth to us'.

Tyrone's name will be spoken in our home. I will acknowledge and mark our anniversaries with wisdom, grace, compassion and respect for myself, my husband, and our family. I have decided that Tyrone's legacy will always be intertwined with mine. The man I chose to marry and the man who chooses me, will be confident in the fact that a part of my heart will always be for

Tyrone however, in choosing to trust in love again, I have chosen to experience and share this different love only with him in entirety. He will not be my "new husband", but a beautiful and integral part of my next page and the only man I will have chosen to be with as I embark on the next chapters of my life. Through honour, respect, communication, intentionality, empathy, compassion, wisdom and a whole lot of patience, among other factors, I believe it will work out with the right person, one hundred percent. Whoever he is, he will be the right person, as I am definitely not for anyone or everyone.

To the Church and Faith Groups

For those of us in the Church, we know what the scriptures say about the love and support which should be shown, especially when it comes to a widow. The Church is called on to play a pivotal role in a widow's life and her processing, healing and restoration. The covering and honour she receives from the Church plays a pivotal role in her ability and confidence to create and establish a new identity as well carry on and continue to carry out her assignments and purpose, especially now that the spiritual covering of her husband has been removed.

Wouldn't it be wonderful if a widow experienced bereavement counselling from a spiritual perspective, delivered by someone she knew and trusted? Wouldn't it be wonderful for a widow to be contacted by leaders who were just checking in to see how she was, especially on significant dates and times of the year which may be particularly difficult, such as anniversaries of weddings, his death, Valentine's Day, birthdays, and during the Christmas season?

Why not have specific leaders trained to deliver this bereavement support as an extension of their existing professional qualifications and expertise? Why not outsource

Chapter 18: A Widow's Call

bereavement care awareness training for all leaders, regardless of the roles of support they occupy in the church or faith group and ensure this training is carried out before the need arises, whenever possible? Do consider assigning women to check in on her over the phone, as well as visit her in person. As leaders, this is your responsibility, which can only contribute to the positive culture of the congregation. Seek to create an environment in which the widow not only hears and receives the love of Christ, but she will learn to open up her heart and love again.

Do consider setting up a care, well-being, or support team if you have not already put this into place in your church or faith group. This can look however you like in line with your vision. I suggest giving specific consideration to appointing leaders who have demonstrated a heart of compassion, empathy and patience with a natural ability to relate and build relationships with others. These could be leaders who work with similar groups of people in their everyday lives, for example, in the spheres of education, social care, family support, counselling and youth work.

These people can be the "front line" for wellbeing and support in your church or faith group, delivering support in the form of check-ins, hospital and home visits. They should have the responsibility of identifying those in need of support and provide initial support and signposting for those requiring extensive support from external parties. There are people who have walked similar paths as me who will be more than happy to provide guidance and support in your church or faith group in the assessment, development and implementation of this support.

In the interest of transparency, even though I attend church, and I am in a position of leadership, there are many days when fear tries to rear its ugly head in so many forms. As mentioned in previous chapters, early on, I was made aware of the battle for my mind. I do not say this lightly — it has taken every inch, breadth, depth and width to protect my mind and not submit to the challenges attempting to invade my mind. I have to daily and intentionally check-in with myself to ensure that I am okay while reminding myself that hope exists; the battle is real.

To the Church, may I kindly request that assumptions are not made based on how a widow presents herself, for example since she appears to be strong and keeps a smile on her face, she isn't still processing grief on her journey and because she was bereaved years ago, she is or should be over it? I assure you that the death of her husband is likely to remain in her heart, and she will never be over it. Even though it has been many years, seasons such as Christmas and celebrations such as weddings and the welcoming of new babies are likely to be somewhat challenging for her.

May I kindly request that the widow be included when teaching and discussing themes concerning relationships and marriage? Whether or not she is currently a part of your church family, do include her in your teaching outside of the context of how Ruth met Boaz. If she is a part of your church family, be aware that although she can relate to a lot of what you teach and share, her ability to access it is different as she has already experienced marriage. Differentiate the topics so she is able to access the curriculum, achieve and make progress as she might in an educational setting. Senior leaders, do consider training and equipping marriage ministry leaders to be able to relate to and adequately support those who have been widowed, mentally, emotionally and socially, as well as those considering or are ready to embark upon a new journey with someone else.

Do continue to embrace and favour the widow, just as Jesus consistently instructed and seek to find out how she is doing as often as possible when she is with you. If she is a part of your ministry's leadership team, please check in with her and foster environments in which she can be honest and feel safe to be transparent about her journey, her walk as she serves and the challenges she faces.

To Community and Support Groups

Where are the young widow support groups in the UK? I start with this question because, as a young widow in the UK, it has been an interesting journey to navigate, not to mention as a young widow in London and more specifically, a young BAME widow in the UK. Throughout my journey, I have sought bereavement support as a young widow however, it seems as if most of the widow support groups — especially those for young widows — are in the USA. Being a young widow, especially one of faith who is open to share her journey, does not seem commonplace in the UK.

I have accessed and received widow bereavement support from two wonderful organisations in the UK however, if I am being completely honest, one of the reasons I didn't continue to engage with support is because I didn't feel I could relate with the people in the room. Yes, I could relate to other widows in terms of the similarity of our grief's journey and the impact it had; however, I did not meet anyone who was from a similar ethnic background, family, or community structure to myself. You might wonder if that really has an impact on an individual's ability to access and engage. I can only speak for myself and my answer would be *yes*.

My first call to action is to the BAME community. Why are death and bereavement still perceived as taboo in the year 2020? We really need to start having open communication about this, so we're knowledgeable and equipped to support others in our families and communities rather than stay away from it.

To community groups already providing bereavement support: thank you because, without your support in the early part of my journey, I wouldn't have had the strength to take my next steps to embrace life after Tyrone. May I kindly request that you assess and tailor your support to ensure that people from all walks of life with different cultural and family backgrounds are able to access your support? In addition to the support already provided, might you consider bringing in a professional from the BAME community to support the differentiation of your resources, tools, leadership training sessions and support events? Can you link to specific individuals and groups in major cities — such as my home city of London — to offer training so they will be equipped to carry out the work and support in their local communities?

PERSONAL MUSINGS:

From Pain to Purpose — Story of a Modern-day Ruth

My greatest fear while married was losing my family.

After one year and nine months of marriage, my husband was diagnosed with cancer.

Seeing my husband in so much pain ripped me apart. I had to be strong for him, for us, for our future. When cancer attempted to emasculate him, I reminded him daily that *he was still my king.*

We were unrelenting in our faith. We completely believed that he would get better and live. Four months later, *my greatest fear* came true: my husband died.

It doesn't make sense that my husband is no longer here. I've been angry with God:

"You have the power to keep him here, why did you take him? We were good Christians! We believed in your Word! We trusted you right to the end! "You were meant to be my Father — why have you done this to us...to me?"

I remember lying in bed a few days after my husband had passed, empty.

I told myself that I wouldn't get out of bed for work, friends, anyone; however, I *would* get up to speak to people about God's goodness. I would actually *get up and go*, in spite of how I felt.

Purpose called out to me and I answered. Under the weight of grief, I decided to get up, follow in Ruth's footsteps and:

Go wherever God leads me! His people will be my people and He will remain my God!

This has been the hardest journey of my life, one on which I feel too young to have embarked.

I have wrestled the dark cloak of depression off of me!

I have wept alone on my floor.

I have experienced financial hardship.

I have suffered intense loneliness.

Those who were meant to be there weren't there.

I look around me and there are new beginnings: marriages and children and businesses being birthed.

I choose to look forward and go into the field. In spite of all this, I choose to move forward. I am prepared to go "into the field" and into the world so I can be used by God to reach those that are deemed "unreachable".

I am seen as a widow, a dark, ugly image of sorrow, an outcast in the field.

Life taunts me, reminding me of what I no longer have in the field

But I still continue.

Biblical Ruth was also bereaved of her husband, but she stayed faithful and believed in the one true God.

I have experienced great loss, but my story isn't over! *I refuse for my story to be over!*

Just like Ruth, I choose to believe that God is still faithful. Yes, I long for my Boaz, for my own family, but for now, I hold onto Hope.

I have gone from *pain to purpose.*

CHAPTER 19:

Tyrone's Dream — The Parable within Parables

I remember this dream in which I was strolling by the wayside of a field and there wasn't anything growing there but for unhealthy-looking flower sprouts and grass shoots with hardly any roots to anchor them in the overturned soil.

Thorns and thistles roamed rampant, choking the space of the smaller and less fortunate seedlings without contemplation, consideration, or care for their botanical cohabitants.

It was truly an unruly sight — there was no discipline or cohesion though the plants shared the Sun's light by day and stared at the Moon by night. They merely existed and they weren't actually living a wholesome life.

I remember seeing a farmer tending the good ground of the field, meticulously inspecting his crop. He spoke, sung sweetly and whispered different things to the ears of each identical plant as if they were individuals. He plucked out the intruding tares, pruned and clipped the branches of the vines with his surgical sheers and sniffed the rapidly blooming fruit borne of each plant.

Unlike the wayside there was order inside the field. Each plant had inherited or received its own lot, visibly divisible from the next plot. There was nothing out of place, the soil was rich and water was provided in intervals through sprinklers along with the natural rain.

Such a scene was evidential proof of the forces separating the wayside and the good ground. In all of my observations, there was one thing I missed: I did not realise that the farmer beckoned me, calling me to come to him and stand in his midst while on my stroll. He guided me to a gate, the proper entrance of His field and greeted me at the opening. He wore a dazzling smile on his face, said, "Hello," and asked, "Are you okay? Do you feel weary and heavy-laden?"

I replied, "I do feel a bit fatigued from my stroll along the wayside and I haven't really eaten."

He said, "Let your heart not be troubled, for here, in my field, you have found your rest. For as I have tended to the needs of the field, each plant is never left wanting. All nutrition and such shall be provided for you, nothing stale, everything always fresh. All I ask is that you refrain from toil, for I do all the labour. Just believe that I can do it all, as I did before you came here to experience my favour."

"I awoke from the Dream, a Sunflower by my bed and Grace knocking at my door, parables within parables on my mind as I shared everything I saw in my dream with her." —
Tyrone Mitchell

CLOSING DEDICATION

Tyrone Anthony Ian Mitchell, there really is no one else that has lived, does live, or has yet to live to whom I can dedicate this book. This book represents a part of your legacy; thank you for being a part of mine.

I know you're looking down from heaven, beaming with pride when you see me. I know you're constantly tugging on Jesus's arm, saying, "Look — look at your beautiful daughter. Isn't she amazing?"

I wouldn't be the woman I am today without having met you. I wouldn't be the woman I am today if I hadn't married you. I wouldn't know what I truly deserved as a queen if I hadn't married a king like you. I truly know my worth because you have taught it to me.

Through you, I understand God's love for me. It took your graduation into heaven to truly understand God's heart as a Father towards me. I am so honoured that out of all the virtuous queens in the world, you chose me with whom to literally spend the rest of your life.

Tyrone, I will forever keep pushing forward to complete my race. How can I give up when you never gave up? I will forever open my heart to love in spite of the possibility of being hurt. I will be patient and forgive quickly. I will continue to see hope glint in the darkest of night skies.

I will forever trust our Father's ultimate plan for my life, one that includes your heart being knitted up with mine. Oh, how I look forward to seeing your mesmerising smile, hearing that thunderous laugh of yours and seeing your eyes light up once again.

As I run towards you on pavements of gold, the first words I will utter are, "Thank you." Thank you for praying for me on every part of our journey when I lived as Maria

Olupeka, and you lived as Tyrone Mitchell. Thank you for praying for us during our beautiful, short-lived journey as the Mitchells. Thank you for praying for me now. Thank you for never judging me when I shared my darkest failings with you. Thank you for being my safe place when I was broken.

Never in my mind did I ever expect to be writing this. It feels as if you left a lifetime ago, yet at the same time, it feels like it happened just the other day. It's a surreal feeling and a vivid reality in a world that continues on.

Your death, the countless tears I've cried and the brokenness I have experienced will never ever change my belief and trust in our Father. It has been the hardest two years of my life. Every part of my being has been tested, yet I still press forward. I will continue to do so with the utmost grace, compassion, and resilience and with a heart that boldly dares to love another again.

Given all I've been through, I am well equipped to run through a troop and leap over any wall! You actually married a warrior! Thank you for being a part of my destiny and my legacy. As you already know, your life and death were not in vain. You left a powerful legacy, one your family, friends, loved ones and even strangers feel, see and hear every single day.

I am doing really well and I'm actually excited about my future. YES!!! Just as I boldly declared in the hospital on the 30th September 2015 in front of our friends, family and pastors: our God is still and will always remain faithful! This is now my life's declaration!

Your light will always shine through my heart and the hearts of others and we will always love you.

Tyrone Anthony Ian Mitchell — until we meet again.

EPILOGUE:
My Love Letter to the Widow

My dear sister and friend, I want to create a space here to speak directly, from my heart to yours.

Though I am a widow, I cannot fully comprehend how much your heart has broken and what has gone through your mind. You have made the choice to read my story for a special reason, and for that, I am eternally grateful. You may relate to a lot of what I have shared, or you may not relate to any of it; however, I ask that you do not dismiss my words, but hold onto any part you feel may have a positive impact or benefit for you and your journey ahead.

I will share my experience of the term, "a widow's heat", otherwise known as the intense desire you may have for physical intimacy after your husband has died. I remember this term being shared with me around a year after Tyrone had died, when I attended a young widow/widowers' retreat and had the opportunity to share how I had been feeling with an ordained minister for the first time.

I had been feeling this intense desire to be physically intimate with someone because I was no longer receiving love in that way from my husband. The minister listened intently and with love and in grace. She explained to me that my feelings were normal and nothing to be ashamed of. She informed me that it was something many women experienced after losing the person they loved. She went on to share that although it is experienced by many, it was a topic and a part of the journey of bereavement that wasn't spoken about much, especially by Christian women.

Although my desires didn't disappear, our conversation encouraged me to seek out a greater understanding of the impact losing Tyrone had (and would have) on me. I understood that I was partially feeling the way I did to numb out the pain. I'd had enough of feeling undesirable, empty and alone. I needed something or someone to take it all away and make me feel better, even if it was for a moment. She helped me to normalise my desires and I no longer felt ashamed of how I felt. The conversation enabled me to be present with myself and honest with God. From there, I was able to put emotional and physical boundaries in place to ensure I didn't make decisions that I would later regret or which would have a negative impact on me in the future.

I share this specific experience because I came to understand that I desperately yearned for my husband and felt robbed of our intimacy. I missed our expression of love and I missed how desired, sought after and safe I felt when I was with him. Although many wild, wild thoughts crossed my mind early in my widow's journey, I made the decision to abstain from sexual intimacy outside of marriage.

What motivated me was that I didn't want to settle for a grief-fuelled interaction after I had experienced such beauty and love within my marriage. I was encouraged when I started to walk closer with God and chose to focus on what I still had and what I had gained rather than what I perceived to be lacking as a result of Tyrone's no longer being around. Yes, it was excruciating and extremely lonely at times and it took all of the strength I had at that time; however, I am glad that I stood by my decision.

At the beginning of my journey, I remember expecting those closest to me to understand how I felt, to say the right words of comfort and be present in the way *I* expected them to be. I learnt that this wasn't entirely realistic for a number of reasons: those closest to Tyrone and me were also grieving his absence and this brought about great pain and sadness. Some expressed the belief that it was better not to say anything than say what might be perceived was the *wrong* thing. Some used physical distance for reasons I still and may never understand. These experiences broke my heart once again, as I felt like I was experiencing what is termed a secondary loss, especially when it came to the breakdown of my most precious and integral friendships.

If you can relate to or have otherwise endured painful experiences in your friendships and relationships, I am sorry you had to go through this in addition to the heartbreak of no longer having your husband physically by your side. You may never understand why this has happened, but please allow yourself a safe physical and emotional space to grieve, process and forgive.

The world will — intentionally or unintentionally — insist that there is a certain timeframe in which to grieve, that grief really only impacts you very early on in your journey and once a certain timeframe has elapsed, your grief needs to stop. To be honest, I experience moments of grief that still pop up, even five years into my journey. One of my favourite discoveries as a new widow was coming across *Tonkin's Model of Grief* (Dr. Lois Tonkin, 1996), which acknowledges and suggests that grief doesn't always disappear with time. Rather, your life grows around the grief. You will have new experiences, meet new people and have new successes as you embrace each day. The grief and the pain of your husband's passing will always be there, though it may not always feel as painful as it did in the beginning because you are growing around it.

In addition to a strong shoulder from trusted friends and loved ones, do ask for as much help as you need from people who are reputable and who you can trust. Where to access support is something I haven't really shared with many people and it is a part of my journey I have chosen not to share in explicit public detail. I think this is because growing up as African, there was always a taboo surrounding death. Even when I was newly widowed, I was encouraged not to share so openly with those who loved me and who were the closest to me. Early on, this made me feel like the death of my husband and my experience surrounding it was a dark, shameful secret in need of hiding. Because I had not learnt how to separate myself from what happened, this affected what I understood to be my identity in a negative way.

It was in a room of counsellors, my first counselling experience eight months in and the second experience sixteen months in as a widow, that I learnt that grieving and processing the grief in my own way is okay and not something that I should be ashamed of. It was in this room that I truly felt listened to and understood. It was in this safe space that I was told that I was strong, and my experiences did not diminish who I was but added to my essence and worth. Even as recent as a year and a half ago, I sought additional support from a relationship coach who supported me as I re-visited my historical pain, challenged false beliefs and learned to take ownership and responsibility for loving myself first. Because of this support, I believe I am now better equipped to continue on my journey of self-love and understand the importance of showing up for myself.

My first Christmas as a widow was bittersweet, as it was also when my younger brother got married. To be honest, the wedding wasn't tremendously difficult for me because I can look back and say I was quite numb, as it was only a few months after Tyrone had died.

What would have been our third-year wedding anniversary was one of my most difficult times because there were others celebrating their anniversaries, but I could no longer celebrate ours. I had planned to mark the first year anniversary of Tyrone's death with friends and we had a lovely time marking that date with an action-packed day and a dove release. Looking back, I feel like I did not plan it entirely for myself, but for the others in attendance. I went into organisation-mode and although it was a beautiful day of remembrance and celebration of his life, I feel as if it wasn't exactly what I wanted or needed for myself, nor was it what I needed to experience at that moment.

Since that first September after Tyrone died, I have spent what would have been Tyrone and my special dates, treating myself to my favourite perfume and body massages and spending Christmas alone in Switzerland. I learnt that it wasn't about what I chose to do, but the fact that I owned my plans and created the space in which to demonstrate love towards myself and create new memories. Though the moments of remembrance over the years have become more private, I have made the decision to mark these precious dates, even if I am alone in doing so.

I urge you never to allow yourself to feel shame for choosing to remember and celebrate *him* the way you choose. Stand up for your beliefs and your *why*, and never feel as if you have to conform to anyone else's ideal or standard of *why* and *how* you should remember him. Even those closest to you may not understand or support your choices and this is okay. Your decisions and actions will always be in your best interests if you carry them out from a place of love towards yourself and others.

In closing, I want to remind you that although you may not feel like it, you are as beautiful now in your heart, mind, emotions and expressions as you were when you were single and when you were married. You are not just listened to, you are heard, even in the moments when you sit alone on your bed or the moments when you're too exhausted to utter words. Your tears have been collected and recorded and they are not in vain as each tear brings you closer to healing. As you continue to believe that your tomorrow can only be better than your yesterday, you will be built-up, and through this journey, you will discover great reservoirs of strength.

As you choose to set your focus and hold onto hope in the midst of this darkness, you will make out the glimmer of light and purpose once again. It may not make sense, but I stand with you as a sister and friend to believe that somehow, the beauty of life will once more radiate from your journey. Follow the voice that says, "You are loved, accepted, and never alone." Follow the voice that says, "I am so proud of every step that you take." Follow the voice that says, "You have everything inside of you to keep going." The dream may not be as perfect as you remember; however, do remember that widowhood is and always will remain a prominent chapter in your beautiful, unfolding story.

Near or Far, I am so proud of the woman you were, the woman you are and the woman you will become. I stand with you as your sister and I will pray for you, always.

With love,

Maria Mitchell

ACKNOWLEDGEMENTS

I was initially against acknowledging specific individuals; however, as I continue to write this book and reflect on key events occurring pre- and post-diagnosis and the initial days and months afterward, I'm not just reminded of God's faithfulness but the faithfulness of a handful of key people. These are people that, if they were not present, I would not be spiritually, emotionally, mentally and possibly physically alive today. I call you my lifelines.

Although we've grown and may have transitioned, you will always be my heart. I love you with every part of me. Thank you for your protection, honour and service.

My Mum — Emily Balogun — and my Family

As a family, you stood on God's promises and interceded on our behalf for a full recovery and beautiful future ahead for me, Tyrone and our family to come. When Tyrone died, I know it did not just break my heart, but it broke yours, too and it was — and still is — extremely painful because you loved him as your own son and brother.

Mum, you are the only person who understands the reasons behind why I asked for my Isaac many years ago and you completely understand what being married to Tyrone and our hopes of a family meant to me. I, therefore, know this has been one of the hardest experiences of your life — to watch your only daughter's heart shatter to pieces as she embarked on the journey of widowhood.

We do not understand the reasons behind what and why things have happened over the years yet I do know it is because of a mother's prayers that my spirit is still alive. You have been patient with me, served me, covered me and battled on my behalf. I always say that if it weren't for your prayers, I have no idea where I would be and we both understand what this means. Mum, you have given me the greatest gift and for that, I am eternally grateful.

Dear Pastor Chido, Pastor Vanessa, and my Radiant City Church family,

Pastor Chido, Pastor Vanessa, and the leaders of Radiant City Church — God positioned you in Tyrone and my lives as a representation of His love and hope. On that Wednesday afternoon when Tyrone died, I asked you never to allow me to forget God's faithfulness. Throughout the years, you always remind me of this every time we speak.

You have been the epitome of God's love in my darkest of days. Even when words could not be articulated, the Holy Spirit interceded on my behalf. You have loved and covered me consistently, as God promised would happen. Through you, God has continually expressed his heart for me. Thank you for being the key anchor that has rooted me in God's love from the beginning. Because of this, I was able to stand and walk again, knowing, somehow, I would be okay.

Pastor Chido — I stayed with the ministry office because of your example. You are a true pastor; thank you for releasing the Father's blessing as I transitioned to my new home: Light London Church. Thank you for always reminding me of God's faithfulness. I am eternally grateful to you, Pastor Vanessa, and the church's prayers.

Dear Apostle Tobi, Prophetess Nicola, and my Light London Church family,

Prior to going to Light London, I had always heard from God. I knew His voice, and I knew how to communicate with Him. It was only after sitting at your feet that I understood the importance of communion with my Father as a friend.

I came to you and into Light London as a woman, a young, tired widow who was hopeful but had little direction. I knew who I was and who I was meant to be; however, I didn't know "how" and "when". I was ready in my heart, but I wasn't equipped.

Apostle Tobi and Prophetess Nicola — you have taught me it is possible to love and war at the same time. You've taught me that generals are called to charge forward in grace. Because of your teaching, I have become more tenacious in nature. I have learned there is power in authenticity, consistency and true submission to the cross.

Under your leadership, I have come to understand that death is just the beginning and that the cocoon, the pit, the wilderness, and the valley are beautiful places. Thank you for loving me and reminding me of eternity. I am honoured to have you as my spiritual covering. Thank you for being a conduit of faith, hope and love, fortifying and commissioning me into destiny.

Dear Renée,

You are my "in the beginning". You are the only one that has walked closely with me from the days I dated Tyrone, through our engagement and as my bridesmaid. Most importantly, you were at the hospital to see Ty and I as we battled. You held us up and loved and honoured him with your words, actions and presence. When he left us, you left your home to sleep in mine. You held me as I wept. You held me as I died and carried me as I came slowly back to life. Even when they found a lump in my breast months after Tyrone had died, you went with me to the hospital and supported me in that frightening time. You have always sat with me and my raw emotions and nothing I shared scared you. You are here now. Tyrone loved everyone, but he trusted only a few. I vividly remember Tyrone asking you to look after me as he laid in the hospital. You promised you would and you have been faithful to your word in every single way. I love you and Tyrone adored your craziness. Thank you for honouring his trust in you. Thank you for honouring me.

Dear Arthur Yafesi,

You are my beautiful story of redemption. Only you and I truly understand what that means. Only those closest to Tyrone and my individual and collective journey will understand.

Arthur, I remember the day I went to collect my results from the hospital. I remember walking to work and crying on the phone to you because I had just about given up on my purpose to love. I was on the verge of giving up on God, but you held me up spiritually. You were my key anchor. You commissioned me not to give up and you made it your duty to ensure I didn't do so. Even when I hated the truth of your words, I listened because I knew of your foundation in God and I trusted your heart where I was concerned. I never ever imagined we would get through the earlier seasons in our relationship, let alone find ourselves here. In the craziest way, you ended up being one of Ty's brothers and closest confidantes. You sat with me as we exercised Ty's legs and ensured he never gave up. When he was tired, you literally carried him. In you, he found the strength that only a brother could provide. You were the one I called to rush me to the hospital that night. You were also the one to hold me tightly as I wept when he died. You have been a sure foundation of my heart and life.

Out of everyone, you were the person that reminded me God was to be trusted. Because of you, my trust in God still stands. I'm so grateful to God for the foundation he built between us in the season before Tyrone came along and I wouldn't change any of the experiences we shared. Thank you for handling Tyrone's heart with such care and covering mine. Thank you for always speaking to the king in him, even when he saw himself as a pauper. Thank you for urging me not to give up on love. Thank you for never giving up on me.

Dear Amanda,

You are one of my oldest friends. You are literally one of the few people with whom I could pick up the phone after not speaking to you for months and we would carry on from where we left off. Thank you for your consistency, reassurance and for always opening your home to me. A few weeks after Tyrone passed, you held me when I went through the hardest few days of my journey. You have been consistent in your love throughout the fifteen years I have known you. Over the last few years, one of the highlights of my journey has been continuing our tradition of coming together every half term to eat rice, stew, plantain and apple crumble and drink Supermalt (I have no idea where this arrangement came from, but I love it). When I think of you, Brian and the boys, I can only aspire to be an amazing mum like you. Thank you for representing the unity, commitment, and friendship of family so beautifully: this representation has literally kept alive my hope for a family of my own. I love you.

Dear Reza,

Also known as my mum's youngest. I have no idea when my mum adopted you as her son, but I definitely know why.

I remember when Tyrone first introduced you as his brother. Tyrone told me that he loved you as he loved himself and his role in your life was to ensure that he showed you love and that he was always there for you. As we know, Tyrone had many brothers; however, there were few that he held in his heart. Reza, you were one of them.

I love you with all I have and from the very depths of my heart. Not many people know this, but our wedding would not have been possible without you. If we ever needed anything, you were there, every time. Tyrone and

I often used to reflect on who you were and how beautiful your heart was. We were proud to call you a brother, our safe place and our confidante. Thank you for your endless sacrifice and ensuring I went without nothing. Heaven remembers every seed you sowed in Tyrone's life, our marriage and my life.

Although Tyrone is no longer with you in person, he was so proud of you, is still your biggest cheerleader and is always praying for you. As Tyrone was there for you, I promise that I will always be a representation of God's love in your life, reminding you that where there is life, there is hope. You are one of life's greatest gifts to Tyrone and me and you will always be loved and cherished. You will always have a safe space in our home as our younger brother and son. We love you.

Dear Chisom, Ethan, Tiana, Sophia, and Olivia,

Chisom — I know that out of all of Tyrone's friends and family, his death hit you differently. I saw glimpses of the brotherhood you shared and I know it meant everything to both of you. Most people were aware of who Tyrone was and what made him happy, but only a few of you had the opportunity to engage with him the way you did. You were heaven's gift to him in the form of not only another brother or a friend but a real-life play buddy. Tyrone was at his happiest when he was by your side, shouting over the console or engaging in your endless Marvel/DC discussions. In your home, with you and your family, he was free to be himself unapologetically. The first glimpse I had that Tyrone would make a great father was when I saw him with your children. He was so proud to be Tiana's godfather and he took his responsibility seriously and loved her and her siblings as if they were his own.

I can never fully understand the impact Tyrone's death has had on you; however, please know that in life — and even in physical death — he adored you, and he was so proud of you as a brother, friend, husband and father. Thank you for your constant kindness towards me and for allowing me to continue being part of your family. Thank you for keeping his life and memories alive in your home and with the children. I know that I may not be as humorous as Tyrone, nor do I have the same interest in comics and computer games as he did; however, you will always have a sister in me.

Dear Rex and Anita,

Anita — I adore the stories you tell me about Tyrone working at the Crown Court and the time when he informed you that he had met the woman of his dreams before asking you to help him choose my engagement ring. This provides a glimpse into the intimate relationship you had with Tyrone as a sister and the relationship you would go on to have with me. You didn't know me yet, but the love you had for your brother allowed you to open up your heart to me when you and Mummy gifted us with the most stunning wedding floral arrangements. After we were married, Tyrone and I spoke about our role models and the couples up to which we looked up to and the couples to which we wanted to draw closer. You were one of them.

Our foundation as a family was really proven when Tyrone passed. I am not sure of the conversations you had with him before he married me, but when we were married and when he was unwell, you both loved and served me unconditionally while expressing that it was the least you could do. Over the last few years, you have gone through your own journeys, yet through it all, you have honoured one another and stood by each other's sides.

Just like some of the others I have celebrated here, we've all commented on the idea that Tyrone placed me in your arms and ensured that I was a part of your family before he departed. Thank you for consistently being my safe place in which I can be completely broken and never made to feel like my love, loss, pain and grief were too much. Thank you for consistently holding a space full of attention and without judgement. Thank you for celebrating me and expressing the words, "We are so proud of you, Maria." You don't know how many times these words came at just the right time. Thank you for being two people to whom I can turn for any need I could ever have.

Thank you for trusting me with your hearts. I love you with all that I am and I can never have enough words to express my gratitude. I am proud of both of you and I celebrate you as a family. Your boys are my boys, and we will always love and celebrate all of them. My symbol of God's redemptive love.

Dear Jenaé and Kwesi,

I can never forget the first time I met both of you. It was about a week before your wedding and a few weeks before our own. I believe Kwesi hadn't seen Tyrone for a long time because as soon as you saw each other, you brought out the old-school stories of childhood antics, music and basketball, including the fact that you, Kwesi, had been the person to introduce Tyrone to Christ. Although we couldn't attend your wedding, not only did you attend ours, but you blessed us by performing your beautiful spoken word piece My Eve.

We started with My Eve and ended saying Farewell. It doesn't make sense that we would come full-circle in only two years.

Until today, I don't believe I've been aware of the cost and level of sacrifice you have made on my behalf. As my representatives, not only did you speak when I had no words or strength to express myself, but you shielded me and covered me from the start, as well as throughout the journey. Oh, how I could not have made it through without both of you. The strength I walk with today is due to the people who have worked tirelessly on the foundation to make sure I would be okay in the weeks, months and years following. You did this for me. From the depths of my heart, thank you for always holding me up with the greatest honour in private and public.

Dear Marc, Suheli, Alina, and Ezra,

Marc, as you are aware, you are the friend I talk about in "Chapter 12: Heavenly Graduation", whom I called in the early hours on that Monday morning to carry out CPR to resuscitate Tyrone after I was told he had died.

Though we only really developed a friendship with you when Tyrone was unwell and in the hospital, you have truly become my family. Marc, you left your wife and six-week-old daughter in the early hours to support me in the hospital and stayed there with me. As a man, you immediately covered me, brought me into your home and took me in as your sister. People can only imagine how it was in the days and weeks after Tyrone had died but you didn't have to imagine it because you walked it with me.

Su — when I think of the positive and beautiful parts of my journey, I think back to visiting you once a week, when you would listen to me process and cry with me, allowing me to rest on your couch when I was tired, and feeding me when I was hungry. Although many people kept their distance from me as the situation was "uncomfortable", you and Marc drew closer. You allowed me to hold Alina as if she were mine, not knowing that your love and embrace contributed to my initial preservation and subsequent healing. You were present the first Christmas after Tyrone died and you held me as I wept outside Westfield shopping centre when the Christmas lights and songs reminded me of what I no longer had. Whether eight-thousand, three-

hundred and fifty miles away in South Africa or a few miles down the road, you and your families have been present and you have wrapped me in your loving embrace. You will forever be wrapped in my heart.

Dear Niel,

I do believe one of the reasons that Tyrone lived as long as he did was due to his commitment to building his legacy. You were the person with whom Tyrone dreamed and planned the vision on a daily basis. Tyrone was so excited about the conversations you had and he couldn't wait to execute them with you. Thank you for believing in the perceived impossibilities and your commitment to the vision. Thank you for honouring Tyrone in life and death and for always celebrating his legacy. When I speak about lifelines, you, Niel, have, indeed, been one for me. Something as simple as the bi-annual gatherings at your home have provided me with continuity as it was something Tyrone and I had attended together. These times of open fellowship have really provided me with the safe place I needed to heal and grow. Knowing I have the opportunity to meet with everyone each year really keeps Tyrone's memory alive in our hearts. Thank you for being a trusted brother to Tyrone and me over the years and for being an intentional friend.

Dear Chi-Lin and Priscilla,

Your intentions and consistency amaze me, even today. Tyrone absolutely adored you both for how open and honest your hearts were to him and others. I cannot write these acknowledgements without writing about you both as you have been a safe place for my heart to rest. Thank you for your endless encouragement along the journey. Thank you for creating opportunities to embrace, experience and enjoy life again. You are both appreciated and celebrated.

Dear Emmanuel Daré Anthony,

I am sure I have previously shared this with you. Before we met, I did not believe men and women could be friends due to my negative experiences and the stories I have heard from others. What I mean by that is that I did not fully believe that a man could be in a woman's life, in close proximity, with the only intention of demonstrating love. I didn't believe it because I had not experienced it until I met you.

You came into my life after I had lost Tyrone. God knew I could not have embarked on this journey the way I did without someone like you in my life. I always joke that you literally know a million people, but the grace in your life allows you to be intentional with each and every one of them.

When I was commissioned as a pastor, the prophetic word that came forth was that I would connect with Aaron and Hur, who would hold my hands up so that they would remain steady until sunset. When I received that word, I thanked God immediately because one of the positions had already been filled in you.

People remark on how strong I am, but only a handful fully know the cost of the seed I have sown, how drenched my pillow has been from the tears I have wept, what my heart looks like when it is completely shattered and how close I have come to giving up on life and hope.

In God's ultimate grace and love, He placed me in your life and you in mine as he knew what was to come. Hand on my heart, I refuse to believe I would have carried myself with such grace in public if I didn't have you to battle beside and run this race with me in private. In correction, in encouragement, in intercession and in your deep embrace, you have demonstrated God's unequivocal love beyond articulation, seeing me for who God says I am.

Whenever I attempt to articulate the way God covers my life, it always looks like you. Emmanuel, you have been the man in my life that has stepped up and consistently covered my heart since Tyrone died. You are my brother, my comrade, my confidante and my pastor. Thank you, Emmanuel, for carrying my heart with full integrity and without compromise.

Dear Mamie,

What can I say about you?! What's interesting is that we became friends after Tyrone died. God knew that I would not have been able to embark on the journey to come without you in my life. You have been a steadfast rock over the last four years, holding me up with your love, wisdom and prayers. You are one of the few people who are aware that Tyrone's death has not been the only heart-breaking part of my journey and with each step I took towards the future, you have been present to guide me forward. My prayer warrior sister, thank you for always reminding me of how precious I am. There have been many days when I felt worthless and forgotten and you would say, "You really do not know how beautiful you are. If only you could see yourself the way I see you." These words have been a lighthouse, teaching my eyes to see beauty again and my heart to love myself again. Thank you for your endless sacrifice, as I know that walking so closely with me on this journey has cost you. I look forward to celebrating God's faithfulness with you. I love you with all my being.

Xavier, Midori, Sally-Ann, and Cutty,

Xav, I actually left the writing of this acknowledgement until last as I couldn't bring myself to write to you and your family. This section is meant to focus on bringing attention to people who have been integral to my life, have contributed to my journey and thanking them for their support. This recognition is fitting for most, but it doesn't do justice to the gift that you are, the position you held in Tyrone's heart and life from childhood until the day he departed. The way you loved him and me and our families is beyond words. Words of appreciation are not fitting. There is nothing on this earth I could ever say or give to express the way you loved Tyrone as a dearest brother, son and friend.

Sally-Ann and Cutty — you lost a son on the 30th September 2015. That day had a drastic impact on your lives, an impact that even I, as his widow, cannot fathom. I want to use these lines to share that Tyrone loved and honoured you with every part of his being. He also loved being a part of your family. As our family, you all fought tirelessly to ensure Tyrone and I received the best care and this gave me the most precious last moments with my dear husband. Thank you for looking after him and contributing to the amazing man he was.

To Xavier, Tyrone's best friend and our best man — although Tyrone did not live to return the favour of being your best man, I know he is so proud of you and he rejoiced with you as you stepped into your new role as husband to beautiful Midori. Thank you for your presence and for being our best man — from the beginning, during our marriage, in the hospital room and to today. Thank you for being someone who Tyrone and I could lean on for anything we needed. Thank you for being his confidante and for holding his heart throughout the years with such care. Midori, thank you for loving me as a sister and welcoming me into your family with open arms. Thank you for caring for Xavier as he walked his journey. Although he is no longer here with us in person, I promise I will keep his name and memory alive and will always share his legacy. He will be forever loved and never forgotten.

In closing: I may not have mentioned you by name; however, I know that I am the woman I am today because of your strength, your sacrifice and your love. Whether it was before I met Tyrone, while he was alive, or after he died, I want to express my heart's gratitude for the part you played in both our lives. Tyrone died knowing that he was loved and he continues to live, expressed through your smiles, words, prayers and actions. I appreciate you and love you, dearly.

AUTHOR BIO

Following the death of her husband, Tyrone, to cancer in 2015, Maria used her personal experience and professional expertise to support bereaved families and individuals who have lost loved ones. As a result of her journey, she is now a trained family support worker and bereavement-counselling supporter.

Maria continues to be an advocate for widows, providing a voice and presence in society inclusive of the church, education and the community. She is passionate about dispelling and challenging myths and shedding the stigma surrounding death, bereavement and grief. She has spoken on Premier Christian Radio and at the Radiant City Church, London, where she continues to authentically and passionately share the intimate parts of her journey as a young widow.

As a commissioned pastor at Light London Church under the leadership of Apostle Tobi and Prophetess Nicola Arayomi, Maria — along with a team — also oversees baptisms and delivers care and well-being support, welcomes new visitors and supports new members.

Audacious and unapologetic in her stance and approach, Maria believes her journey through widowhood — inclusive of the challenges and trials — has resulted in an unexpected and distinctive beauty, greater awareness and appreciation of self as well as a greater resilience. She truly believes and stands by the motto: *what the caterpillar perceives as the end, to the butterfly, is just the beginning.* She believes that life can come after death, that death does not need to be the end, but a redirection and invitation to embark on a different course and a beautiful beginning.

Conscious Dreams
PUBLISHING

Be the author of your own destiny

Find out about our authors, events, services
and how you too can get your book journey started.

- Conscious Dreams Publishing
- @DreamsConscious
- @consciousdreamspublishing
- Daniella Blechner
- www.consciousdreamspublishing.com
- info@consciousdreamspublishing.com

Let's connect

www.ingramcontent.com/pod-product-compliance
Lightning Source LLC
Chambersburg PA
CBHW021114080526
44587CB00010B/516